# GROWING HEALTHY HOUSEPLANTS

## Choose the Right Plant, Water Wisely, and Control Pests

Ellen Zachos

D0094616

Storey Publishing

*The mission of Storey Publishing is to serve our customers by
publishing practical information that encourages
personal independence in harmony with the environment.*

Edited by Sarah Guare and Carleen Madigan
Series design by Alethea Morrison
Art direction by Jeff Stiefel
Text production by Theresa Wiscovitch
Indexed by Christine R. Lindemer, Boston Road Communications

Cover illustration by © Meg Hunt
Interior illustrations by Beverly Duncan

**Storey Publishing**
210 MASS MoCA Way
North Adams, MA 01247
*www.storey.com*

Printed in the United States by McNaughton & Gunn, Inc.
10  9  8  7  6  5  4  3  2  1

LIBRARY OF CONGRESS CATALOGING-IN-PUBLICATION DATA

Zachos, Ellen.
  Growing healthy houseplants : choose the right plant, water wisely, and control pests /
by Ellen Zachos.
    pages cm. — (Storey basics)
  ISBN 978-1-61212-440-7 (pbk. : alk. paper)
  ISBN 978-1-61212-441-4 (ebook)  1.  House plants.  I. Title. II. Series: Storey basics.
SB419.Z32 2014
635.9'65—dc23
                            2014028774

# CONTENTS

I can't imagine living in a home without greenery, but 20 years ago I feared the houseplant, convinced I'd kill any I touched. I'm not sure why I was so afraid, since I'd never actually tried growing anything, but the whole idea seemed very mysterious and intimidating.

Then one day, when I was doing a show in Florida (my first career was acting), a friend gave me a peace lily as an opening-night gift. That simple houseplant changed my life. It brightened up my rental condo for the run of the show, and when the play was over I carefully packed it in my carry-on luggage and brought it back to New York City. I didn't understand the joy I felt with the unfurling of each new leaf, but I knew I wanted more — so much more that eventually I left the glamorous world of show business to become a professional gardener.

If I had a nickel for every time someone told me they couldn't grow houseplants, I'd have at least 50 bucks. The truth is that my thumb is no greener than anyone else's. If you can follow a recipe or assemble a bookcase, you can grow houseplants. Here's my recipe for success:

1. Accurately evaluate your light (page 5).

2. Choose a plant that suits your light (pages 85–118).

3. Apply the right watering techniques (page 14).

4. Sit back and watch it grow.

It's important to start with low-maintenance houseplants because success breeds success. Once you've experienced how easy it is to garden indoors, you'll want to do more, and before you know it you'll be planting terrariums, propagating leaf cuttings, and installing grow lights. I can see it now.

## Why You Need Houseplants

Houseplants improve the air we breathe. It's an impressive process: Plants combine water and carbon dioxide with sunlight to produce sugars and oxygen. They save the sugars for later, but they generously share that oxygen with us. Some plants even remove pollutants such as formaldehyde and benzene from the air we breathe. That might seem like a sophisticated, technical, scientific accomplishment, but for plants it's just part of their day-to-day, get-up-and-go-to-work routine.

**Houseplants are alive!** And because they're alive, they bring life into your home. The most sterile environment becomes warmer and more welcoming when graced with a living plant. And a windowsill full of foliage and blooms? It's downright energizing. It's easy to add plants to every room in the house. An herb garden in the kitchen is a tasty decoration. Sprouting an avocado seed with your child adds life to her play space and teaches her about nature. A fern in the bathroom takes advantage of the humidity left over from your morning shower. And an elegant palm is a graceful addition to any living room.

**Houseplants are decorative.** You've got a personal style, and your plants communicate that style. What you choose to grow (and how you choose to grow it) says something about your aesthetic and reveals your creative side. And here's the beauty part: if you decide to redecorate, changing your houseplants can give a whole new look to a room. A fragrant jasmine is stimulating and sensual; it says you enjoy both exotic blooms and strong perfumes. An architectural sago palm tells the world you appreciate living sculpture and strong form. A trailing ivy is the perfect choice for a country kitchen, where its classic shape complements traditional decor.

**Houseplants are inherently optimistic.** Okay, the plants themselves aren't optimistic, but having them in your home makes *you* optimistic because growing plants means you're looking toward the future. You anticipate each new leaf and every bloom, and rejoice in each success.

**Houseplants make a house a home.** Remember that rental condo in Florida? It was generic, filled with someone else's wicker furniture and abstract oil paintings. My peace lily changed all that, adding a personal flourish to my temporary digs. Feather your nest with foliage and flowers to create a personal space for yourself, your family, and your friends.

Indoor gardening satisfies the human desire to nurture a living thing. It's an easy and inexpensive way to unleash your creativity, have fun, and do something with your own two hands. You can do it on any scale, in any style that suits you. Take a deep breath, and let me show you how.

# LEARN TO SPEAK PLANT

Before we dive into indoor growing in all its glory, you need some basic vocabulary.

What's in a name? Scientists have given all living species (plants, animals, insects) their own two-part Latin names, known as binomials. Some gardeners resist using Latin names, claiming they're hard to pronounce and highfalutin. Alas, if you want to be sure you're getting exactly the plant you're looking for, you must use Latin names. Not only do common names vary from place to place, but one common name may be used for different plants. If you're dying for a pot of coralberry and order it as such, you may end up with either *Ardesia crenata* or *Symphoricarpos orbiculatus*. There's a big difference.

    A plant name is composed of a genus, plus either a species or a hybrid name. If the plant is unique, it may be given an additional cultivar name to distinguish it from other plants of the same species or hybrid. Hybrids may be naturally occurring or man-made. A cultivar is always man-made. Sound confusing? Let's think about plant names in terms of cars. It's really not so difficult.

## A Key to Understanding Latin Plant Names

|  | GENUS | SPECIES OR HYBRID | 'CULTIVAR' |
|---|---|---|---|
| **Definition** | A group of plants classified together because of common ancestry; can be man-made or naturally occurring | A further division of a genus and a closely related group of plants; a hybrid is an offspring resulting from crossing two species | A single genetic representation of a species or hybrid |
| **How it's treated** | Always capitalized; either italicized or underlined | Species are not capitalized and are either italicized or underlined; hybrids are always capitalized and not italicized or underlined | Set off in single quotation marks |
| **Car example** | *Honda* | Odyssey | EX |
| **Plant examples** | *Ficus* | *bennendijkii (species)* | 'Alii' |
|  | *Saintpaulia* | Fantasy (hybrid) | |

# TROPICAL PLANT VS. HOUSEPLANT

MOST PEOPLE DON'T REALIZE that many common houseplants are tropical plants. You say "tropical plant" and people think exotic, fussy, and difficult to grow. Well, that couldn't be further from the truth. If you've ever grown a spider plant, a pothos, or a weeping fig . . . you've grown a tropical!

What's the difference between a tropical plant and a houseplant? A houseplant is any plant you grow successfully in your home. A tropical plant is any plant native to the tropics (the part of the earth located between the Tropic of Cancer to the north and the Tropic of Capricorn to the south). Most of our houseplants are actually tropicals, which makes a lot of sense when you think about it. So let's think about it.

## A Tropical Environment

In the tropics, the sun is basically directly overhead throughout the year, which makes its light intensity uniform. In temperate zones, the angle of the sun changes greatly from season to season. This means that light intensity is much greater in temperate summers than it is in temperate winters.

The sun's angle also affects a location's temperature. Because the sun is directly overhead year-round in the tropics, temperatures do not fluctuate as widely as they do in temperate regions. The temperature in Cancun is 80°F (27°C) in February and 90°F (32°C) in August. In Chicago, the difference between average summer and winter temperatures can be a whopping 60 degrees Fahrenheit (33 degrees Celsius).

And finally, day length in the tropics is essentially the same year-round, while in temperate climates you may get 15 hours of daylight in summer and a mere 9 in winter.

So how does this relate to growing tropical plants as houseplants? Well, your living room feels just like the tropics . . . as far as your plants are concerned. It doesn't snow; the temperature is generally between 55 and 80°F (13–27°C); and there are approximately 12 hours of light per day (counting light from lamps), of even intensity.

## Are All Houseplants Also Tropicals?

While most houseplants are native to the tropics, there are a few subtropical plants that are also well suited to being grown indoors. The earth's temperate zones are located between the tropics and the Arctic and Antarctic Circles. The term "subtropical" is used to describe the warm regions adjacent to the true tropics. While light frosts occasionally occur in these areas, they are rare. "Mediterranean" climates and citrus-growing regions of the United States are both considered subtropical, and some plants native to these areas make excellent indoor plants.

Conversely, many of our favorite temperate garden plants do not make good houseplants because they require a winter dormancy of several months with temperatures below freezing. Some also need a long, uninterrupted period of darkness. Those are not conditions you're going to want to replicate in your living room.

Whether you choose tropical or subtropical plants as houseplants, the most important thing is to pick plants that grow well in your home. Consider temperature, light, and other idiosyncrasies of habitat before experimenting with a new plant species. The more you know about the way a plant grows in nature, the better your chances for successful indoor gardening.

# PART ONE

# ESSENTIALS

Give your plants a few basics and they'll be happy. Good light, adequate water, and nutritious soil are all they really need.

## LIGHT: HOW MUCH IS ENOUGH?

IF YOU'RE GOING TO UNDERSTAND only one thing, it should be light.

How much light does a plant need? That's the first, most essential question you must ask yourself before bringing any new plant into your home. If you can't give it the light it needs, the plant is doomed. Doomed, I tell you!

Often, houseplants will be labeled low-, medium-, or high-light plants. These may sound like grossly general categories, but they're actually pretty helpful.

- **Low light:** Northern exposure; obstructed eastern or western exposure; room interior
- **Medium light:** Eastern or western exposure; this may be either bright, indirect light or a few hours of direct sun
- **High light:** Unobstructed southern exposure; 6 to 8 hours of full sun

Of course, nothing is cut and dried. You'll have to decide for yourself whether the blue spruce in front of your west-facing window turns your sill into a medium- or a low-light location. Every growing situation is individual, but the above categories give you a place to start.

How do you further define what kind of light you've got? Choose a method based on your personality. Are you a technophobe? Use the shadow method. If you're an equipment geek, use your camera or buy yourself a light meter. Either way, with time you'll develop a feel for light intensity, and ultimately, you'll be able to judge with your eye alone.

**Shadow method.** The shadow method requires nothing fancier than your eyes and a hand. On a sunny day, turn out all the lights and hold your hand about a foot above the spot (or table) where you want to grow your plant. If you can see a dark, sharply outlined shadow for 6 to 8 hours, you have a high-light location. (You don't have to stand there the whole time, but do

## Changing Places
*You can bend the rules a little by rotating your plants in and out of optimum light. After all, what's the point of getting that begonia to bloom if you can't take it out of its window and show it off as a centerpiece when company comes to call? When the plant finishes flowering, move it back to its growing position.*

check on your shadow every hour or so.) If you see a shadow with slightly blurred edges, you have a medium-light location. A faint shadow with fuzzy edges indicates low light. No shadow at all means you need supplemental light to grow here.

**Using a camera or light meter.** If you want to be more precise in your measurements, you'll need to understand foot-candles. A foot-candle is an approximation of the light given off by one candle at a distance of 1 foot. High-light plants need approximately 3,000 foot-candles, medium-light plants need between 1,500 and 3,000 foot-candles, and low-light plants need about 1,000 foot-candles. That said, plants are highly adaptable creatures and will often pleasantly surprise you by blooming even when light conditions aren't optimal.

If you have a single-lens reflex camera, you can use it to measure foot-candles. Set the film speed to ISO 25 and the shutter speed to 1/60th of a second. Place a white sheet of paper in the spot where you want to measure and place your camera 2 to 3 feet away. Focus on the sheet of paper, and read the f-stop for a correct exposure. Use the chart below to find the approximate foot-candles that correspond to your f-stop reading.

### F-stop to Foot-Candle Translation

| F-STOP | FOOT-CANDLES | F-STOP | FOOT-CANDLES |
|--------|--------------|--------|--------------|
| 2 | 100 | 8 | 1,500 |
| 2.8 | 200 | 11 | 2,800 |
| 4 | 370 | 16 | 5,000 |
| 5.6 | 750 | | |

If this seems like too much work, or if your inner geek secretly wants to buy another gadget, get yourself a light meter that measures in foot-candles. A decent meter will cost between $50 and $100 and will give immediate, accurate readings with the flip of a switch.

## Artificial Light

Let's pretend you failed the shadow test. Even if you get no natural light at all, you can still have an indoor garden; you'll just need a little extra equipment. Before you decide what kind of equipment, consider these three characteristics of light: intensity, color, and duration.

**Intensity.** Light that seems bright to the human eye is not necessarily intense enough for optimum growth of tropical plants. Low light intensity may not kill a plant, but it can result in weak growth with elongated, spindly stems. Without adequate light, plants will not fruit or flower.

**Color.** The sun emits light in all colors of the visible spectrum: red, orange, yellow, green, blue, and violet. White light is a combination of all of these. However, not all colors of light are equally valuable to plants. Light in the blue and red ranges is most important for plant growth. Flowering plants require large amounts of orange and red light to bloom and set fruit, and light in the blue range promotes lush, compact foliage. Grow lights are special bulbs designed to deliver specific wavelengths of light necessary for plant growth.

**Duration.** This refers to the number of hours of light a plant receives per day. Since artificial light doesn't exactly duplicate the intensity and color of sunlight, you can compensate by giving plants more hours of artificial light than they would receive outdoors in their native habitats. Increased quantity compensates for reduced quality, and duration is easily regulated by including a simple timer in your grow light setup.

So what kind of grow bulbs should you use?

## FLUORESCENT LIGHTS

Fluorescent lights are inexpensive and require no special wiring or installation. The most common type of fluorescent tube is the cool white bulb, which emits a bluish light. Warm white tubes emit more light in the red end of the spectrum. Seeds can be started under cool or warm white bulbs, and many foliage plants can also be grown successfully under these lights. Use one of each in a double-tube fixture for a good balance of useful light.

For a little more money, there are special full-spectrum fluorescent tubes engineered to provide light in the wavelengths most useful to plants (the blue and orange/red ranges). To the human eye, the light given off by these bulbs is similar in color to that of the noonday sun. They cast a pleasant light in your dark living room. However, there is some controversy over whether these bulbs are worth the additional expense. Many growers believe that a combination of the less expensive cool and warm white tubes is equally effective. If you are just beginning to experiment with growing under fluorescents, start with the less expensive bulbs and see how you do. If your plants grow well but you don't like the visual quality of the light itself, consider buying the full-spectrum bulbs.

Because fluorescent lights give off very little heat, plants can be placed close to the bulbs (5 to 6 inches) without risk of burning. Fluorescent tubes produce less light at the ends of the tubes than at the center, so plants requiring less intense light should be placed under the 3 inches of tube at either end of the fixture. Fluorescent tubes should be replaced every 12 to 18 months if they are being used approximately 14 hours a day.

## INCANDESCENT LIGHTS

Incandescent grow bulbs are less efficient than fluorescent grow lights, since much of their energy is given off as heat, rather than as visible light. On the plus side, they can be used in many common household lamps, and they are adequate for certain low-light foliage plants. A 60-watt bulb at a distance of 2 feet will provide approximately 20 foot-candles of light. At this low light intensity, growth will not be rampant, but certain low-light species can be maintained under these conditions.

Incandescent grow lights can also be used to boost the brightness of a partially obstructed window, increasing the number of plant species you can grow. Track light fixtures can be fitted with grow bulbs to brighten a larger area. Since incandescent bulbs are hot, don't place them too close to foliage or it may burn. A minimum distance of 18 to 24 inches is recommended.

## HIGH-INTENSITY DISCHARGE LIGHTS

High-intensity discharge (HID) lights are the brightest grow lights available. There are two subcategories of HID lamps:

metal halide (MH) and high-pressure sodium (HPS). Each produces a different color of light determined by the blend of gases contained in the tube at the center of the bulb. You can use a combination of MH and HPS lamps in a single location, but a metal halide bulb cannot be used in a high-pressure sodium fixture, and vice versa (the bulbs have different electrical requirements).

Both metal halide and high-pressure sodium lights emit more intense light than fluorescent or incandescent lamps. They operate with regular 120-volt household current but require special fixtures, so this isn't a bulb you can just plug into your favorite lamp. These fixtures tend to be industrial in appearance.

**HID LIGHTS** produce intense light for indoor growing.

Also, consider the location of your interior landscape as well as what you want to grow when choosing your HID lamp. Metal halide and high-pressure sodium lamps produce very different colors of light, which promote different types of plant growth.

**Metal halide.** These bulbs give off light that is strongest at the blue end of the spectrum. This light produces compact, leafy growth and is preferable when your light garden is an integral part of your home, since the light won't distort the colors of the plants (and people) it illuminates. Metal halide bulbs are less expensive than high-pressure sodium lamps, but they need to be replaced more frequently — about once a year. If you're growing plants mainly for their foliage, this may be the best choice for you.

**High-pressure sodium.** These bulbs last about twice as long as metal halide lamps but cost slightly more per bulb. They emit a strong light at the red/orange end of the spectrum and promote flowering and fruiting. If your goal is lots of blooms, use high-pressure sodium lamps, but remember, their light has a strong red/orange cast and distorts the colors of everything and everyone it illuminates.

### LED LIGHTS

Light-emitting diodes (LEDs) are the newest entry in the grow light market. Large commercial units can be highly effective, comparable to HID lights. Such units are expensive to buy (think hundreds of dollars) but not to operate, since LEDs use very little electricity. Small household LED units have several things to recommend them. Their light is much more intense than that of fluorescent tubes, and they are quite efficient, losing little energy to heat. Plants can be placed close to the bulbs (12 inches) without risk of leaf burn. Their light is attractive, and the bulbs can be used in household light fixtures. Since LED bulbs are spotlights, rather than tubes, they are better suited for single plants or small groups, while fluorescent tubes cover more growing space.

If you're just beginning to experiment with artificial light, start with LEDs or fluorescent tubes — whichever suits your growing space. If you're thrilled by your success, you may decide to invest in an HID system, in which case you'll be able to grow a wide range of houseplants, no matter what your natural light levels are like.

## Artificial Light Uses

| BULB TYPE | RECOMMENDED USES |
| --- | --- |
| Fluorescent | Seed starting; supplemental light; sole light source for low-light plants |
| Incandescent | Supplemental light; sole light source for very low-light plants |
| HID/Metal Halide | Foliage plants; supplemental or sole light source |
| HID/High-Pressure Sodium | Flowering plants; supplemental or sole light source; light has a strong yellow/orange cast |
| LED | Seed starting; supplemental light; sole light source for low- and medium-light plants |

# WATER AND HUMIDITY: GETTING IT RIGHT

WATERING A PLANT SOUNDS LIKE a simple task, but it requires some thought. Over-water and you kill the plant. Under-water and you kill the plant. The symptoms of both can look bewilderingly similar. In essence, what happens is the same. When a plant is under-watered, its roots don't absorb enough water and the plant shrivels and dies. When a plant is over-watered, its roots rot and the plant can't absorb water or nutrients. It shrivels and dies.

It's possible to grow some houseplants without fully understanding the concept of watering; certain plants are quite forgiving of less-than-perfect watering schedules. Casual growers may make lucky guesses, learn a schedule by rote, or depend on devices like moisture meters to tell them when it's time to water. But if you truly understand *how* to water a potted plant, your indoor garden will be healthier and more beautiful. And who wouldn't want that?

## Understanding How to Water

There is no set schedule to memorize, but there are several simple concepts to master. By understanding how a plant uses water, as well as what affects the rate at which water is used, you can assess the needs of each plant in your indoor garden.

Water enters a plant through its roots, travels up through the plant's vascular tissue to the leaves, and is released to the air. This is called transpiration. Water molecules leave the plant's foliage through osmosis — the passage of water from an area of high water density to an area of low water density. This water, in the form of vapor, passes through openings on the underside of plant leaves, called stomata, as a product of photosynthesis.

Everyone who gardens indoors knows that plants need water, but not everyone understands why the amount of water is important, so let's start there. Plants in the ground have a large amount of earth through which their roots extend in search of water and nutrients. Plants in containers have a very limited amount of potting mix from which their roots can draw water and nutrition.

The amount of potting mix in a container determines how much water can be retained. Water molecules adhere to soil particles, filling the spaces between those particles that hold air when the potting mix is dry. When you water a potted plant, the air spaces between soil particles become filled with water, which is then absorbed by the plant's roots over time. A plant needs both water and oxygen, so it's important to find the right balance in your watering schedule. You must allow the soil to dry out enough to provide the plant's roots with oxygen, since keeping the soil consistently damp may make it impossible for the plant to breathe. That being said, some plants have adapted to soggy soils and grow best in potting mixes that are consistently wet.

It is extremely important to water a plant thoroughly each time you water it. I cannot stress this enough. (Seriously: this is the takeaway.) Thorough watering means watering a plant until water runs through the drainage holes in the bottom of the pot. If a plant is bark mounted or potted in bark mix, thorough watering means soaking the entire plant (pot or mount and all) for 10 minutes in a bowl of water. If you water a plant incompletely, you encourage root growth only in the portion of soil that has been watered. This means that roots grow only through the portion of soil that receives moisture, instead of deeply and throughout the pot.

One of the primary functions of any root system is to provide anchorage for the plant. A plant with an underdeveloped root system will be at a disadvantage because it will not have the ability to absorb adequate water and nutrients from the soil, and it will not be well anchored where it grows. If a root system is confined to the top few inches of a container, it is entirely possible for a top-heavy plant to literally pull itself over and out of its pot. I speak from experience.

**SOAK PLANTS** potted in bark mix to allow each piece of bark to absorb as much water as possible.

## Water Cues from Plant Structure

There are numerous ways plants can store and retain water under dry conditions. Some plants have developed a thick cuticle — a waxy layer covering the plant's epidermis. The cuticle creates a barrier between moisture in the plant foliage and the surrounding air, so foliage loses water more slowly via transpiration, and the plant can go longer between waterings. Other plants have thick leaves with storage tissue for holding water in times of drought. Cacti have modified foliage (spines) and specialized storage tissue that allows them to go for long periods of time without water. Conversely, plants with delicate, thin leaves and slim stems lose water more quickly via transpiration.

Look for visual cues to assess your plants' water needs. Even if you don't know what type of plant you have, if it has thick leaves and a shiny, waxy leaf surface, it's a good guess it's a drought-tolerant plant. Peperomias, hoyas, and even some orchids are common examples of succulent, drought-tolerant plants that present these clear visual cues.

## Seasonal Water Needs

You may have noticed that most plants require less frequent watering in winter. This is a function of reduced temperatures and shorter daylight hours. In spring, houseplants begin to grow more rapidly in response to longer daylight hours and warmer temperatures. As their growth rate increases, so does their need for water.

Photosynthesis, a plant's means of producing its own food, can be summarized as follows:

$$\text{Water} + \text{Light} + \text{Carbon Dioxide} =$$
$$\text{Oxygen} + \text{Energy} + \text{Nutrients}$$

For the rate of photosynthesis to increase, a plant requires more water, more light, and more carbon dioxide. Therefore, plants require more water as they move into active growth.

Most houseplants are in active growth from spring through fall. Some, however, are in active growth when you least expect it. For example, while most houseplants require less frequent watering in November or December, that is exactly when a holiday cactus blooms, after a period of cool drought. Your holiday cactus will need increased water at this time to support flowering. Your cue will be when you see the first buds.

## Environmental Influences

Have you ever woken up on a winter morning with a nose so dry you could hardly breathe? Just as dry air robs your mucus membranes of moisture, so does it wick water molecules out of plant tissue. Therefore, warm, dry air increases the frequency with which you should water your houseplants. If you control your own thermostat, consider maintaining a nighttime temperature between 60 and 65°F (16–18°C) and then set it at 70°F (21°C) during the day. Your plants will require less frequent watering and will be less stressed by heat and dryness.

Plants in north-facing windows require less frequent watering than those in south-facing windows. The lower light

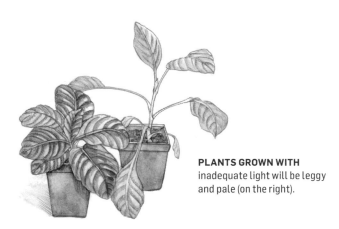

**PLANTS GROWN WITH** inadequate light will be leggy and pale (on the right).

and temperature of northern exposures results in slower photosynthesis and transpiration. High temperatures and light levels increase a plant's need for water. When these demands are met, the plant is able to grow more rapidly and well. If a plant doesn't get enough light and water, new growth will be thin, spindly, and pale. If this happens, cut back the weak new growth, move the plant to a location where it gets the right amount of light, and adjust your watering schedule.

If you're growing under artificial lights, be aware that this increases your plants' need for water. Lights generate heat and dry out container soil, and increased light hours speed up photosynthesis and transpiration. The closer the lights are to the plant material, the more frequently you will need to water.

## Container Choice

Did you know that the type of container you choose can affect the frequency with which you'll need to water? Both the size and the material of the pot are significant.

The smaller the pot, the smaller the volume of soil and water it can hold. Therefore, a small pot needs water more frequently, since its soil cannot accommodate as many water molecules as a larger container. In addition, a pot made from a porous material such as clay, wood, or concrete will lose water via evaporation through the container walls, as well as through the soil surface. Containers made from nonporous materials such as plastic or metal will lose water through the soil surface only, so they will need less frequent watering. A porous terra-cotta container becomes nonporous when covered with a waterproof glaze.

Container choice is primarily a matter of aesthetics, but there are practical considerations as well when planting large containers. Large trees or mixed plantings can be prohibitively heavy if potted in clay or wood. Fortunately, there are attractive fiberglass pots on the market that resemble clay and cast cement. They are lightweight and easier to move. Also, being nonporous, they require less frequent watering than their clay counterparts.

If you choose to pot your plants in plastic for practical purposes, you may want to double-pot them in more attractive containers, such as art pottery or wicker baskets. This is an excellent way to combine the practicality of a nonporous pot with the beauty of a unique container.

The key to successful watering is to correctly gauge how *frequently* you must deliver water, not how *much* you should give your plant. Each plant will have its own optimum schedule, but here are a couple of rules of thumb:

- **For houseplants in containers less than 12 inches in diameter,**
  water when the top inch of soil feels dry to the touch. Stick

your finger into the soil, and if it feels dry down to the first knuckle, it's time to water.

- **Large trees and plants in containers more than 14 inches in diameter** should be judged by a different standard. The top 2 inches of soil can feel dry to the touch before these plants require watering.

Over time, you will develop a feel for how often your plants need water. You'll be able to tell from across the room if a plant is thirsty or drowning by the color and turgor (swelling) of its leaves, as well as by its feel. Don't be afraid to get your hands dirty. Stick your fingers in the soil and test the moisture at different levels. Consistent care and attention on your part will always be essential to the health of your plants.

## Paraphernalia

Now that you fully understand everything that affects the frequency with which a plant needs to be watered, it's time to consider how you will water your plants. What tools do you need?

There are several alternatives to the traditional watering can, and you can choose your tool according to your personal style. An indoor hose with a wand attachment can be hooked up to your sink with an inexpensive adapter. Hoses are lightweight and come in many lengths. Some are coiled, like telephone cords, and thus store easily. Wands may be used for watering or misting.

I confess: I'm a spiller. (Ask my husband . . . it drives him crazy.) So I don't water my hanging baskets in place. I have a watering station where I hang plants over plastic wash basins, water them, and allow them to drip-dry before hanging them back in place.

A turkey baster is an extremely useful utensil when performing your regular watering chores. Use it to suck up extra water from plant saucers. Overflowing water can ruin your floor or carpet, and a plant sitting in water is at risk for root rot. A simple baster can help you prevent both of these problems.

Just because it's old-fashioned, don't disregard the traditional watering can. There's a reason it's been around so long. Any good watering can should have a smooth flow of water; a long, narrow spout will allow you to place the water exactly where you want it, without spilling or wetting foliage. Wider spouts deliver a greater volume of water more quickly than narrower spouts, so consider the size of the container you are watering when choosing a watering can.

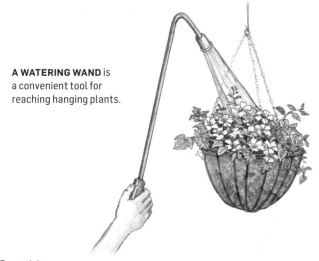

**A WATERING WAND** is a convenient tool for reaching hanging plants.

# Tap Water Cautions

A few chemicals in tap water may harm certain plants. You can remove the chemicals with some simple strategies.

Many communities add fluoride to their water to reduce tooth decay. Unfortunately, some of our most common houseplants are easily damaged by fluoride, including spider plants, ti plants, corn plants, prayer plants, and peace lilies. The foliage of sensitive plants may blacken, with burned-looking leaf tips and margins. Certain specialty filters remove substantial amounts of fluoride from tap water. If your water is heavily fluoridated, consider installing an activated charcoal, reverse osmosis, or distillation filter. These remove between 80 and 99 percent of the fluoride. A potting mix with a high pH level may reduce the availability of fluoride to your plants, but if your water is heavily fluoridated, you may need to reconsider growing some of these more sensitive plants.

Chlorine is not usually present in concentrations high enough to damage plants, but certain species such as *Tradescantia* are particularly sensitive. Many water filters remove chlorine from tap water; you can also let your tap water sit for 24 hours, allowing the chlorine to escape. This has the added benefit of warming your tap water to room temperature. Cold water shocks roots and over time can stunt growth and weaken the general health of your plants, making them susceptible to disease. Cold water on leaves can even cause foliage spots. Human beings may not relish a drink of tepid water, but your plants will prefer it.

## Elevating Humidity Levels

Some tropical plants require the high, fog-up-your-glasses humidity of a greenhouse, but many will survive in average household humidity. If you don't have a greenhouse but would like to try growing some high-humidity plants, there are several ways to elevate humidity levels in your home.

You already know about transpiration — the process of water being released as vapor through the plants' stomata as a by-product of photosynthesis. In especially humid environments, some plants exude water through specialized cells at their leaf tips in a process called guttation. Both transpiration and guttation raise the humidity of the air immediately surrounding the plants. By grouping plants together, you can increase local humidity. As each plant releases water (as vapor or as liquid), the relative humidity of the air increases. This will both reduce the frequency with which you need to water and provide a more tropical humidity level for your houseplants.

Another simple solution is to create dry wells for your plants. A dry well is a tray or saucer of pebbles where your plants sit. Most of your plants are probably already on saucers, which catch the overflow of water. You can either add a layer of pebbles to individual plant saucers, or use a large cookie sheet with pebbles to hold several plants in a single spot. Keep the pebbles covered with water, just up to the level of the bottom of the pots. As the water evaporates from underneath and around the pebbles, it humidifies the air around the plants. If the water level is higher than the bottom of the pot, this could lead to root rot; don't let that happen. Be sure to use plastic saucers or trays made from nonporous materials. A clay saucer will let moisture pass through to the floor below and could lead to stains or warping.

I don't recommend misting your plants to raise humidity. This is basically a waste of time. The humidity boost lasts only as long as it takes the water to dry, so unless you plan to quit your job so you can stay home and mist your plants, you're better off creating a few dry wells.

**DRY WELLS** are the easiest and most efficient way to raise humidity for your plants.

# THE GROWING MEDIUM

GARDEN SOIL IS NOT RECOMMENDED for potting houseplants for several reasons. First of all, it's heavy. Soil weight is an important concern, especially when planting large containers. Someday you may want to move that 8-foot *Ficus* in the 24-inch pot to another room, and if it's planted in heavy soil you'll be very, very sorry. Garden soil may also contain harmful pathogens such as insects and fungi. And finally, garden soil dries out more slowly than commercial potting mixes. In a large, nonporous container, garden soil could stay too wet too long, leading to poor oxygenation of the soil.

## Potting Mixes Aren't Just Dirt!

Bagged potting mix comes in two basic types: soil-based and soilless. Both are sterile and suited for indoor gardening.

**Soil-based potting mix.** If you grow moisture-loving plants, consider using a soil-based potting mix. It retains water longer than soilless potting mix and drains more slowly, decreasing the frequency with which you need to water. Prepared potting soil differs from ordinary garden soil in several ways: It is composed of sterilized, loamy soil; sand/perlite/vermiculite; and peat moss. The pH may have been adjusted for optimum growing, and both macro- and micronutrients are sometimes added.

**Soilless potting mix.** Many commercial potting mixes are actually soilless; these will be labeled "pro-mix" or "professional potting mix" rather than "potting soil." They are lightweight and well suited to growing many houseplants. Soilless mixes drain quickly. Peat moss is a common ingredient and is used both for its light weight and its ability to retain water and nutrients. However, when peat moss dries out completely, it becomes hydrophobic (difficult to rewet). As a result, soilless mixes composed entirely of peat may be too lightweight and not retain water well. When shopping for a container mix, consider its ingredients carefully. Look for a combination of peat, perlite and/or vermiculite, and bark.

**Custom potting mix.** Certain plants require special potting mixes. Some cacti grow well in a soilless mix, but others are happiest in a soil/sand combination. Epiphytes (plants that grow in trees, like many orchids and tropical vines) should be grown in a super-fast-draining potting medium, such as a bark mix. The large particle size of bark mixes guarantees that epiphyte roots get the excellent aeration they require.

Creating a custom mix is simple. If you keep a few basic ingredients on hand, you'll be able to mix up a batch of exactly

---

## *Potting Mix Recipes*

- **All-purpose:** 3 parts bark, 1 part peat moss, 1 part perlite
- **Cactus:** 1 part perlite, 1 part sterilized soil, 1 part sand
- **Moisture-retentive:** 2 parts peat moss, ½ part perlite, 2 parts sterilized soil
- **General epiphytic:** 2 parts bark, 2 parts peat moss, ½ part horticultural charcoal, 2 parts perlite

---

## Moveable Plant Stands

*Plant stands with casters and wheels can be handy for moving heavy potted plants, but be sure to get a model that's strong enough for your plant. A large tree needs a sturdy wooden stand; plastic won't support that kind of weight for long.*

what you need. Start with the horticultural equivalent of Bisquick (not from scratch, but not ready-made, either). In other words, find a bagged mix you like and tinker with it, adding bark to make it drain more quickly or sterilized soil to make it retain water longer. Once you've gotten the feel of it, you can try composing a potting mix from scratch.

## FERTILIZATION: MORE ISN'T ALWAYS BETTER

FERTILIZATION IS ESPECIALLY IMPORTANT to understand for container growing. Plants have only a small volume of potting medium from which to draw nutrition, and several components actually have no nutritional value whatsoever. Peat does not contribute nutrition to potting mix, but it does a great job retaining both water and nutrients. Perlite does not contain nutrients, but it is used to aerate potting mix. Bark can also be used for aeration purposes, since the large size of the bark pieces creates a coarse mix. Both bark and soil contain nutrients in various stages of decomposition.

The more frequently you water your plant, the more rapidly nutrients will leach from the mix. For this reason, you can't rely solely on the nutrients in your potting mix — you will also have to feed your plants. Even the most nutrition-packed medium will eventually have its unconsumed nutrients leached out through repeated watering.

All fertilizer packages are marked with three numbers, which represent the percentage (by weight) of three macronutrients: nitrogen, phosphorus, and potassium. Nitrogen promotes healthy, green foliage; phosphorus supports flower and fruit production; potassium assists with root development.

## Types of Fertilizers

There are three main types of fertilizers to consider: balanced, high nitrogen, and bloom booster. Each of these types of fertilizers can be further divided into organic and nonorganic varieties, and most are available in water-soluble or time-release granule form.

**Balanced.** A balanced fertilizer contains equal amounts of each of the three macronutrients and encourages all-around growth. The package is marked with three equal numbers (for example, 5-5-5 or 10-10-10).

**High nitrogen.** Some plants have special nutritional needs. For example, an epiphyte potted in a bark mix may require extra nitrogen. Bark decomposes more slowly than soil, releasing less nitrogen to the plant's roots. In this case, use a fertilizer that has a higher first number (30-10-10, for example).

But be aware: this high dose of nitrogen can promote foliage growth at the expense of flowers.

**Bloom booster.** If your plant isn't blooming the way you think it should, try feeding it with a "bloom booster"— i.e., a fertilizer with a higher percentage of phosphates (and a formula with a higher middle number, such as 5-10-5). African violet food is by definition a bloom booster and can be used for a wide range of plants.

**Organic.** Organic fertilizers tend to have lower numbers (such as 2-2-2), but that doesn't mean they're not as good. Most houseplants don't need a lot of extra nutrition. Truth is, plants make most of their food through photosynthesis. Fertilizers provide essential nutrients for plants in the same way a multivitamin does for humans. You don't need the vitamin if your diet is perfectly balanced, but if you eat like most people, you could use a little extra help. If your plant has less-than-perfect soil and growing conditions (and that's a given, because it's growing in a small pot in your living room, not in a tropical rain forest), then it will benefit from a little extra nutrition.

**Water soluble.** Water-soluble fertilizers are easy to deliver. They can be added to water and given to your plant when you water. You can soak plants in a solution of fertilizer and water (especially good for epiphytes potted in bark-based mixes), or you may spray a fertilizer solution onto the leaves with a mister. This is called a foliar feed, and it's a quick, direct way of getting nutrients to your plant. If you choose a foliar feed, make sure you spray early in the day so any liquid left standing on the leaves has plenty of time to evaporate. Standing water at cooler nighttime temperatures creates a breeding ground for plant diseases.

**Time release.** Time-release granular plant foods are convenient for gardeners but not so great for plants. Since these granules dissolve slowly, over time, nutrients are concentrated in the top layers of soil rather than distributed evenly throughout the container. And if your plant is potted in bark, fertilizer granules may fall through the spaces between bark pieces.

## How Much?

I think most people over-feed their plants, and I think most plant food labels encourage this over-feeding. After all, they're trying to sell plant food. If you use a balanced liquid fertilizer at half the recommended strength every other week during the growing season, that's plenty. Less is okay; more is not. For most of us, the growing season begins in early spring and continues through early fall. If you notice buds forming, leaves emerging, or stems lengthening, the plant is in active growth. During the winter months, you don't need to feed most plants at all.

It is entirely possible to kill a plant with kindness; over-fertilization can be deadly. A white crusty buildup on the edge of your pot or on the surface of the mix indicates that the fertilizer salts are not being fully flushed from the container. Too much fertilizer can burn the roots, which results in foliage damage and eventually can kill the plant. If you notice this type of buildup, stop fertilizing your plant and repot with fresh mix. With fertilization, it's better to err on the side of too little rather than too much.

# PART TWO

# DAILY CARE

A little bit of attention on a regular basis keeps your houseplants happy and healthy.

## COOL TOOLS YOU'LL NEED

INDOOR GARDENING isn't a tech-heavy hobby, but there are a few tools you *must* have and a few more that will make your life a lot easier.

**Bypass pruners.** My first gardening teacher told me I should buy the most expensive tools I could afford. I thought he was nuts, because who doesn't love a bargain? When my second set of cheap pruners bit the dust after a few months of heavy-duty use, I realized he was right. It may hurt to pay out $50 for a pair of pruners, but they'll last your whole life (I'm at 16 years and counting) and end up costing less than a new $5 pair every year.

There are two basic kinds of pruners: bypass pruners and anvil pruners. Bypass is better. Anvil pruners cut by bringing one sharp blade down on top of a flat blade. It crushes what it cuts, which is fine if you're cutting up twigs and branches to throw away. However, if you're pruning a plant and you want it to keep growing, it's better not to crush the stem. Bypass pruners have one sharp blade that slides past another sharp blade, cutting a stem without crushing it.

Design is important, so try different styles to find one that fits your hand well. Some have rotating handles, some are designed for smaller hands, some have ratcheting blades for extra power. Then when you've chosen your pruner, buy yourself a holster. It's *so* worth it! It's much harder to misplace a tool when it's attached to your body.

**Floral snips.** You might wonder why you need floral snips when you have a great pair of pruners. Floral snips are designed to fit into tight spaces and are perfect for removing delicate flowers and making cuts between branches that are too close together to accommodate the wider profile of a pruner. They

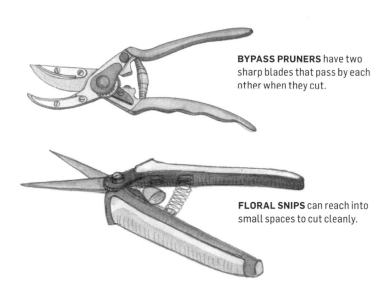

**BYPASS PRUNERS** have two sharp blades that pass by each other when they cut.

**FLORAL SNIPS** can reach into small spaces to cut cleanly.

also double as scissors. You may need to cut a piece of string or open an envelope of fertilizer, and pruners are ill suited to these tasks.

**Turkey baster.** Sooner or later it's bound to happen. You'll empty a watering can full of water into a plant, only to realize (too late) that it's *way* too much water and the saucer is bound to overflow, staining your carpet and warping your floor. If the plant is small, you might be able to carry it to the sink without spilling and pour the extra water out of the saucer just in the nick of time. But if the saucer in question is underneath a 4-foot palm tree, well, good luck with that. Use a turkey baster to suck up excess water and squeeze it out into your watering can. Disaster averted.

**Trowel.** Trowels are great multitaskers in the indoor garden. Obviously, you'd use one to transfer potting soil from the bag to the pot. But a sharp trowel can also be used to open a bag of potting soil (better than pruners!) and a sharp blow from a trowel can transform a clay pot into a batch of pottery shards (who needs a hammer?). Again, try a few different models to see what's most comfortable for you: wooden handle or molded rubber? Wide blade or narrow? The choice is yours.

**Gloves and glove clip.** Some gardeners like to work in gloves, others don't. It's a personal choice, mostly dependent on which is more important to you: clean hands or feeling the details of what you're touching. If you're pro glove, I highly recommend a glove clip. Gloves tend to come off and go back on a lot (you answer your phone, you eat an apple), and I lost many pairs before I realized I should just clip them to my belt loop.

**Spray bottles.** Spray bottles are useful tools, but probably not for the reason you think. Remember, they are not an efficient way to raise humidity for your plants. Spray bottles are great, however, for delivering a foliar feed to your plants and for applying pesticides, but be sure to keep separate bottles for fertilizers and pesticides — and mark them clearly.

**Pruning saw.** If you grow indoor trees such as weeping fig or citrus, you may occasionally encounter a branch that's too big for your pruners. While you might be able to use a pair of large loppers (from the outdoor tool shed), a pruning saw is a more precise instrument. It fits nicely into the fork of a tree and is less likely to tear bark when it cuts.

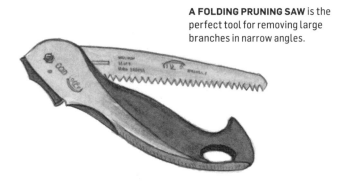

**A FOLDING PRUNING SAW** is the perfect tool for removing large branches in narrow angles.

**Potting tray.** A potting tray made from hard plastic keeps your work area neat and, more importantly, dry. Some come with attached shelves and tool compartments, but even the simplest design makes cleanup a lot easier at the end of a repotting binge.

**USE A POTTING TRAY** to keep your work area clean.

**Magnifying glass.** Some plant pests are hard to see with the naked eye. A magnifying glass is a handy diagnostic tool.

**Cotton swabs, cotton balls, rubbing alcohol.** If you pay attention to your plants, you won't have much need for heavy-duty insecticides. But every once in a while you'll spot a mealybug or scale insect that requires immediate removal. Most of us already have cotton swabs and cotton balls on hand, and these are perfect for wiping down foliage and swiping off insects. Keep a few on your potting bench along with a bottle of rubbing alcohol.

# REPOTTING: IT HAS TO HAPPEN SOMETIME

IN NATURE, PLANTS HAVE lots of room to spread their roots in search of water and nutrition. In a pot, access is limited to a small volume of soil, so we compensate by giving the plant regular water and food. You will also occasionally need to repot your plants, giving them fresh soil and more room to grow.

How do you know when it's time to repot a houseplant? Here are some questions to ask yourself:

- Are roots poking out from the drainage hole in the bottom of the pot? They're not trying to escape . . . they're just telling you they need more space.
- Are roots circling the soil at the top of the pot? Again, not a jail break, just a signal that the roots are out of room.
- When you water your plant, does water immediately run out of the drainage hole? If so, there isn't much soil left in the pot. As roots grow, they gradually displace soil. You hardly notice a few particles here and there, but they add up.
- Has the plant been in the same pot for more than 3 years? Does the soil smell a little funky? The structure of the soil particles breaks down over time, and nutrients are exhausted. Fresh soil will give your houseplants a little boost.
- Does the plant look too big for its pot? In general, it should accommodate the rootball and top growth with room to grow but without leaving vast expanses of unused potting soil. More on this later.

- Does it tip over easily because the top growth is heavier than the ballast provided by its roots? A larger pot with more soil adds weight to the base of the plant.

If you answered yes to any of these questions, it's time to repot. Lots of indoor gardeners are intimidated by the idea of repotting. I know I was. I put off repotting my clivia for so long that the roots actually cracked the pot. They might as well have been screaming, "Let me out of here; I can't breathe!" Let me talk you through a few simple steps so you won't make the same mistake.

## Repot When the Time Is Right

*If your plant is in flower, you should wait to repot even if there are roots poking out the bottom. A plant in flower needs all its energy to promote bloom. Recuperating from a transplant might make the flowers drop prematurely by drawing energy to the root system.*

# HOW TO REPOT

## 1. FIND THE RIGHT POT

First, choose a container one size bigger than your current pot. Pots come in standard sizes, usually in 2-inch increments. A 6-inch pot is a pot with an interior top diameter of 6 inches. The next size up would be an 8-inch pot, and that would give a 6-inch rootball a full inch of fresh soil all the way around.

Resist temptation to move your plant into a *much* bigger pot. You may think you're saving yourself time because you won't have to repot the plant so often if you move it into a big pot now, but over-potting can kill a plant. If you moved a 6-inch rootball into a 12-inch pot, that would give the rootball 3 inches of fresh soil all the way around.

Why would that be a bad thing? After you water a plant, the soil gradually dries out as the roots absorb water from the soil. This balance between wet and dry, oxygen and water, is crucial (as I'm sure you remember from chapter two). Fresh soil with no roots in it will stay wet, surrounding the rootball with moisture, keeping the roots wet for longer than they should be. The roots may rot, killing the plant, slowly, in front of your very eyes.

## 2. REMOVE THE PLANT

Find a pot *one* size larger than your current container, and have a bag of potting mix (see chapter three) and a pottery shard (a broken piece of an old pot) or small piece of landscape cloth or screen. Cover the hole in the bottom of the pot with one of the above to keep soil from dribbling out the bottom of the pot, then add an inch or two of soil. Next, knock the plant out of its pot.

To do this, tip the pot upside down, holding the stem of the plant loosely between your fingers. If the rootball doesn't slip right out, knock the pot (hard) against the side of a table, or, if the pot is plastic, roll it on its side while pressing down hard. This should loosen the rootball so you can slide it out gently. It is not unheard of for a plant's roots to attach themselves to the pot's walls. You may need to crack a terra-cotta pot (try a hammer) and peel away the pieces. Or, for a plastic pot, cut it apart with a pair of scissors.

**CIRCLING ROOTS** indicate that a plant is pot-bound.

Take a look at the rootball once it's exposed. An extremely overgrown plant may have roots that completely encircle the plant. If this is the case, poke your fingers in and among the roots with your fingers, teasing the roots apart to loosen them up. (Notice how little room there is for soil?) Use the same strength of touch you'd use to untangle a snarl in your hair: firm but kind.

### 3. REPOT THE ROOTBALL

Place the rootball in the center of its new pot, holding it in place with one hand, then add soil around the edges with the other. Press the new soil in firmly (you may need to use a dowel or chopstick to really poke it down), adding more until the new soil meets the level of the existing soil. You always want to maintain the original potting level of the plant. This should be about ½ inch to 1 inch below the rim of the pot so water won't splash out every time you water the plant.

### 4. WATER THOROUGHLY

Bring the plant to the sink, and water it thoroughly. (I *know* you remember how to do this!) The soil may settle in a little while you're watering. If necessary, add more, pressing it in firmly and watering again.

If your newly transplanted plant looks droopy or wilted, keep it in a shady spot for about a week, away from air conditioners, radiators, or fans. All three of these dry the air. After a week your plant should be perky again. You can move it back to its regular place and resume normal care.

## Top-Dressing

*There are times when you may want to refresh a plant's soil without moving it into a bigger pot. You can do this by top-dressing. Scrape a little potting mix off the top of the plant (an inch is fine), and replace it with fresh soil.*

# GOOD GROOMING

WHY DOES PRUNING STRIKE FEAR in the hearts of otherwise normal human beings? Perhaps it's the sharpness of the tools involved, or maybe it's remembering the trauma of an early childhood haircut. Either way, pruning is a necessary skill for every gardener, and it's a lot easier than cutting your own fingernails. Think of it as good grooming for your plants.

The most elementary form of pruning is pinching, for which no special tools are required. If you've ever walked past a coleus and pinched off a flower stalk or a pair of emerging leaves, you have, in essence, pruned a plant.

Often, we pinch a plant to make it branch. A plant's growth hormones are concentrated in the tip of the stem, and as long as the primary stem of the plant grows naturally, growth hormones elsewhere will be suppressed. When the growing tip is removed, the growth hormones at lower nodes on the plant may become active, causing branches to sprout lower down on the stem. What is a node? It's a growing point on a stem or branch. It can be marked by a bud scar, a bump, or different-colored tissue.

If the plant stem feels woody and you can't easily pinch it with your fingernails, use pruners or floral snips. For small houseplants, a pair of snips is perfect. The small size of the blades allows you to get into tight angles and make clean, professional cuts. Using traditional pruners in very acute angles can be difficult; you can damage stem tissue with the scrape of a blade or by pushing the pruners into a space too small to accommodate them. So if you're working with delicate plants, buy a delicate pair of snips. No matter which tool you use to prune, every cut should be made at about a 45-degree angle, just above a node.

Pruning is a good way to rejuvenate a plant. If new foliage looks unhealthy, weak, small, or damaged, prune it off, correct the problem (too much water, too little light, and so on), and wait for healthy new growth. For example, imagine that during your vacation a neighbor watered your plants. Unfortunately, she moved one up against a window and several leaves suffered damage from the cold glass. Simply prune away the damaged leaves and move the plant back from the glass. New growth should be perfectly normal.

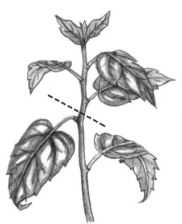

**PRUNE PLANTS** at a 45-degree angle, just above a node.

## Shaping Top Growth

Sometimes a plant grows so well that it outgrows its place, and it becomes a question of either finding it a new home or pruning it to fit the space. If a plant is an old favorite, it's preferable to cut it back and keep it in place. Start slowly, and you won't do irreparable damage. You'll also avoid the psychological shock of seeing a large plant greatly reduced all at once.

Step back from the plant, and look at its overall shape. Where exactly is it too big? Is it touching the ceiling? Is it nudging aside the mirror on the wall? Is it draping over the back of the couch? Start where it is most overgrown and remove about 10 percent of the offending branch. Work around the plant, making sure your work is even, removing approximately 10 percent from any part of the plant that is larger than you want it to be.

Ten percent is conservative, but by starting small you make the job less intimidating. Once you've reduced the size of your plant by approximately 10 percent, take a break. Is it enough, or should you prune more heavily? When you're satisfied with the general shape of your tree, look at your cuts. Are they clean and well placed?

Some plants, including *Ficus*, *Euphorbia*, and *Hoya* species, exude a milky sap when cut. When pruning plants that ooze, lay a drop cloth or some newspaper to catch liquid that could stain furniture or flooring. If you're only making a few cuts, pieces of wet paper towel will stanch the flow.

Thick branches and tree trunks may be too large to cut with handheld pruners. A pair of loppers will cut through wood

1 to 1½ inches thick, and a folding handsaw with a nice sharp blade can handle anything thicker. Pruning limbs of this size on a houseplant is unusual but may occasionally need to be done.

## Root Pruning

Once you've mastered pruning stems and branches, pruning root growth is the natural next step. If a plant has outgrown its pot, but you don't want to move it to a bigger container, root pruning is an option. Knock the plant out of its pot and loosen the soil as best you can. Cut from all sides of the roots, just as you would with top growth. If the plant has been in a large pot (greater than 12 inches in diameter), prune away approximately 2 inches all around the rootball. If the plant is in a smaller pot, prune away approximately 1 inch from all sides of the roots' mass. When the rootball has been reduced, put it back in the pot and fill in around the edges with fresh soil, packing it in as firmly as possible.

In the past, gardeners were taught that after pruning the roots, you should proportionally reduce top growth. We believed that a smaller root system would be less able to pump water and nutrients throughout the plant, and therefore we should reduce the workload for the newly root-pruned plant. We were wrong! What we now understand is that pruning top growth causes a flush of growth that actually increases the amount of water and nutrients the roots need to transport. So after root pruning, do not prune top growth unless there are damaged stems or branches that should be removed. Pay special attention to irrigation as the root system recovers from its surgery. You may need to water a little more often than usual, but don't overdo it.

## Aesthetic Pruning

There are other types of cutting and pruning done for aesthetic reasons. Thin-leaved plants may brown around the edges as the result of over- or under-watering, dry air, or cold temperatures. With a pair of scissors, trim the damaged tissue from the leaf margin, preserving the original shape of the leaf. A pair of sharp scissors is the right tool for this job.

You can dead-leaf a plant using dexterous fingers. Brown and yellow leaves will not regain their original green color, and should be removed. There's no point allowing the plant to expend energy supporting a leaf that is doomed; that energy is best diverted to the strong and healthy growth of the plant.

It's normal for plants to lose their lower leaves as they age. Of course, leggy plants can be rejuvenated by taking cuttings (see page 52), but vines can also be given a new lease on life by clever camouflage of their bare stems.

If you have a vine with long lengths of stem that have lost their foliage, twine the leafless stems around the inside of the pot's edge, then pin the stem to the soil at regular intervals. You can use a paper clip for this: straighten it, cut it in half, then bend it into a U shape. The stem will root along its length and send up growth from the newly rooted stem. Your plant will look as if it has been pruned, but you won't have to take cuttings.

A healthy plant looks good, and an unhealthy plant doesn't. It's as simple as that. Sometimes a light pruning is all it takes to make a plant look terrific, but sometimes a little more work is necessary. Whether your plant needs a simple pinch or a full root prune and transplant treatment, the plant can't groom itself. So be brave, pick up a pair of pruners, and take the plunge.

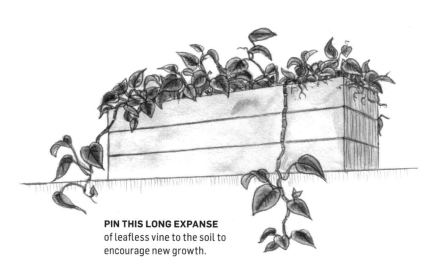

**PIN THIS LONG EXPANSE** of leafless vine to the soil to encourage new growth.

# PROPAGATION: MAKING MORE PLANTS

PLANT PROPAGATION MEANS making new plants from old plants, and it's one of the most satisfying things a gardener can do. It's also a skill that's surprisingly easy to acquire.

There are many methods of propagation, all of which fit into two categories. Sexual propagation involves plants' reproductive parts, such as seeds and spores. If you've ever started a tomato from seed, you've propagated a plant.

Indoor gardeners usually propagate their houseplants via asexual reproduction. This involves vegetative plant parts such as roots, stems, and leaves. Vegetative propagation is faster and easier than starting seeds or spores, and it guarantees you get another plant exactly like the one you started with. So whether you want more plants for yourself or to give away to your clivia-coveting friends, vegetative propagation is a great way to go.

## Separation

The simplest type of vegetative propagation is separation. Many plants produce offsets that can be separated from the parent plant. Both spider plants (*Chlorophytum comosum*) and strawberry begonias (*Saxifraga stolonifera*) produce offshoots at the ends of stolons (modified shoots that grow from a plant). Offsets that form at the ends of stolons can be treated in several ways. They can be left on the parent plant and pinned to the soil with a bent paper clip, where they will root and form new plants. Or they can be separated from the parent plant and potted up on their own. An offset that is allowed to root while still attached to the original plant will need no special care. Once it has established its own root system, the stolon can be severed. An offset that is separated and potted up on its own will require higher humidity and more frequent watering while its root system develops.

Many bromeliads also produce offshoots. However, they grow directly from the stem of the original plant, not from stolons. Bromeliads are monocarpic, which means they flower once, then die. Before dying, a bromeliad produces new plantlets. These can be separated from the mother plant and potted up on their own once they have developed roots of their own.

Orchids also frequently produce plantlets on the stems of the original plant. Orchid offshoots are called keikis, which means babies in Hawaiian. A keiki can be separated from the mother plant and potted in bark mix once its roots are at least 1 inch long.

## Plants That Can Be Separated

- Climbing onion (*Bowiea volubulis*)

- Earth star (*Cryptanthus* spp.)

- Flamingo flower (*Anthurium* spp.)

- Spider plant (*Chlorophytum comosum*)

- Strawberry begonia (*Saxifraga stolonifera*)

## Division

Division is similar to separation but involves some sharp tools. However, if you mastered the pruning lessons on pages 42 to 47, you're ready for this. Plants with more than a single clump or crown, such as peace lilies, flamingo flowers, and elephant ears, are good candidates for division. Plants with a single growing point, such as a weeping fig or citrus, cannot be divided.

If a plant has outgrown its pot, why not try division? Knock the plant out of its pot, and inspect it at soil level. How many individual growing points can you see? If there are two, this plant can be divided into two smaller plants. If you see six, you have choices: you can divide it into two, three, or more small pots. Make your decision based on how large you want the resulting plants to be. On your first try, keep it simple and split the plant in half.

**USE A SHARP KNIFE** or pruning saw to slice cleanly through a rootball.

## Sizing Up Your Plants

*It's important to develop a sense of the proper proportion of rootball size to pot size. In general, if a rootball is 4 inches in diameter, the pot should be about 6 inches in diameter. An inch of fresh soil around the circumference of the pot will allow for new growth.*

You may be able to separate the two pieces with your hands, depending on how dense the rootball is. Hold the soil ball on either side and tug gently. If you can separate them a little bit, work your fingers into the crack, pulling the pieces apart. Continue until you separate the parts of the rootball. It is inevitable that some roots will be broken, so don't worry. Be as gentle as possible without being tentative.

If the rootball is extremely dense, you may have to pull out a sharp knife. Place the tip of the knife between the two growing points, and cut down through the root mass, dividing the plant into two sections. Remove and discard any severed root fragments, then pot up your division in containers of the appropriate size (see box, above).

Keep your newly potted plants out of direct sun, and be attentive to their water and humidity needs. After about 2 weeks, they'll be ready to resume their original positions. If you see new growth before that, congratulate yourself and move on. The more practiced and skilled you become at division, the less traumatic it will be for your plants.

## Plants That Can Be Divided

- Cacti (various jungle and desert)
- Clivia (*Clivia miniata*)
- Philodendrons (various)
- Prayer plant (*Maranta* spp.)
- Squirrel's foot fern (*Davallia fejeensis*)

## Cuttings

Many tropicals can be propagated by cuttings, which is an especially satisfying way to make more plants. Cuttings can be taken from stems, roots, or leaves, depending on which species you're propagating. In each case, it's fascinating to watch new plants grow from pieces of the old.

Propagation from cuttings is based on a plant's wound response to tissue injury. When plant tissue is cut, callus tissue forms. This looks like warty, knotty growth. If you've ever rooted cuttings in water, you may have seen this kind of tissue develop on cut stems before new roots started to grow.

A word about rooting cuttings in water: roots absorb oxygen and nutrients differently from water than they do from soil. Roots that grow in water have a hard time adapting from water culture to soil culture. For this reason, I don't recommend rooting cuttings in water, then transferring them to potting mix. If you'd like to watch how roots grow, by all means, start a few cuttings in water. But don't be surprised if the cuttings don't prosper when they're moved to soil.

Many tropicals root well from stem cuttings. Prepare several small plastic pots by filling them with a lightweight, sterile potting mix, just as you do for seeds. Firm the mixture with your fingers, and poke a hole in the mix for each cutting. If you're using 2-inch pots, one cutting per pot is fine. If you're using larger pots, give each cutting about 2 inches of space to grow.

Stem cuttings should be 4 to 6 inches long and include several nodes. Small cuttings reduce the potential for wilting. The more tender the leaf tissue, the smaller the cutting should be. If the surface area of the leaves is larger than 3 square inches, reduce it by trimming the leaves.

## Which End Is Up?

Plants have polarity, which means they distinguish between up and down. The *proximal end* is the part closest to the crown of the plant and the *distal end* is the part of the cutting farthest from the crown. If you place the wrong end (i.e., the distal end) of a stem cutting in the rooting media, the cutting won't grow. To avoid this, standardize your method. If you always make your proximal cut straight and your distal cut slanted, you'll be able to tell the ends apart. You might not expect this to be a problem, but if you take several cuttings from a single stem it's possible to get confused.

1. Make your cut just above a pair of leaves, then remove the bottom pair of leaves from your cutting. This should leave one or two pairs of leaves at the top of the cutting.

2. Dip the bottom of the stem in water, then in rooting hormone (see box, below), being sure to cover both the bottom cut end and the wounds where the leaves have been removed.

3. Tap off any excess hormone and stick the cutting in the potting mix. Firm it into place, and water the pot.

4. Cuttings don't have the ability to absorb water, and if they wilt, they'll die, so you have to provide elevated humidity while the root system forms. Place small (2-inch) pots in individual ziplock bags, blow them full of air, then seal. If you have a group of potted cuttings, place the group in a large dry cleaning bag, or in a plastic tent. Once your cuttings have rooted, gradually reduce the humidity while the roots begin to take up water.

### Rooting Hormone

*While it is not always necessary, dipping your cuttings in rooting hormone can speed the rooting process. Plants produce hormones naturally, and auxin is the hormone that initiates root production. By applying auxin to the cutting, the rooting process can be accelerated.*

Bottom heat can speed the rooting process for stem cuttings, especially when air temperatures are cool. Remember, raising the soil temperature will cause soil to dry out more quickly, so pay special attention to maintaining elevated humidity if you use a heat mat.

Check your cuttings after two weeks. Tug gently on the top of one; if it pulls out of the mix, firm it back in place and continue to wait. If you meet with some resistance, roots have started to grow. Continue to keep the cuttings in elevated humidity. When you see signs of new top growth, you can remove the cuttings from their shelter and treat them as individual plants. This process can take anywhere from 3 to 8 weeks, depending on the plant.

### AERIAL ROOT CUTTINGS

Some vining plants produce aerial roots along their stems. In nature, these roots hold the vine in place, but the humidity in most homes is too low to encourage aerial root growth. Begin as you would for rooting in potting mix, by taking a 4- to 6-inch cutting. Wrap the cut end in a moist paper towel, and place the cutting in a large, clear ziplock bag. Blow the bag full of air, and place it in a warm, bright spot, not in direct sun. Check the paper towel every few days to make sure it remains moist. If it has dried out, rewet the towel and reseal the bag.

Within 2 to 3 weeks, you will find that roots have grown not only under the paper towel, but also along the stem. Unwrap the towel as best you can. It is not necessary to remove every piece of paper before potting up the cutting. You may

## Plants for Stem Cuttings

- Mosaic plant (*Fittonia verschaffeltii*)
- Crown of thorns (*Euphorbia milii*)
- Lipstick plants (*Aeschynanthus* spp.)
- Stephanotis (*Stephanotis floribunda*)
- Wax plant (*Hoya* spp.)

either plant the cut end in potting mix or pin the length of the vine along the surface of the mix with bent paper clips. Leave the planted cutting in its moist chamber for a few weeks, then adjust gradually.

After two to three weeks, tug gently on the stem. If you meet with some resistance, the roots are taking hold. Keep the plant in its moist chamber for another week, but leave the plastic bag open. The following week, remove the newly rooted cutting from the chamber entirely and place it on a dry well to elevate humidity. One week later, you can move your new plant into place.

### LEAF CUTTINGS

Some houseplants can be propagated from leaf cuttings; rex begonias, African violets, and snake plants are all excellent candidates. For example, a single leaf from an African violet can be removed from the mother plant, the end of its stem dipped in rooting hormone, and the leaf potted up in light-weight potting mix. Within four to six weeks, a new plant will grow from the base of a single leaf.

To propagate rex begonias, remove a single leaf from the plant. Turn the leaf over, and make several cuts across the major veins of the leaf. Pin the leaf right side up on top of potting mix using bent paper clips. Make sure the cuts make good contact with the potting mix. New plants will grow from these points.

A single snake plant leaf can produce many new plants. Cut a single leaf into 1-inch sections, making sure to distinguish the proximal and distal ends of your cuttings. All succulent

**REX BEGONIAS** can be propagated by cutting and pinning a mature leaf.

cuttings must be allowed to heal before being planted; otherwise, they may rot, not root. Dip the proximal end of the cutting into rooting hormone, then place it upright in a soilless potting mix. Plant the cutting as deep as you must to get the leaf to stand on edge. Firm it in place, and treat it as you would a stem cutting.

Because snake plant foliage is succulent, you may think maintaining high humidity is not as important as it is for a tender-leaved plant. But this is not the case. Snake plant cuttings are slow to produce new growth and must be kept in high humidity during this time.

## Plants for Leaf Cuttings

- African violets (*Saintpaulia ionantha*)
- Rex begonias (*Begonia rex*)
- Snake plant (*Sansevieria* spp.)

# VACATION FOR YOU, VACATION FOR YOUR PLANTS

SUMMERING PLANTS OUTDOORS is an appealing prospect for several reasons. First of all, most plants respond to outdoor growing conditions with a flush of growth. Second, it's a lot easier to take care of your plants outdoors. The humidity is already high, so you can forget about dry wells, and you don't have to worry about spilling when you water. Just pour and pour until it runs out the bottom of the pot.

There are a few things to consider. First, that full sun outdoors is *much* stronger than the full sun that shines into the indoors. If you have a plant in full sun indoors, don't move it directly into full sun outside or your plant may suffer from leaf burn. First put your plant in a shaded position, then into dappled light, then into full sun. This way, your plant will have a chance to acclimate. A plant grown in indirect light indoors should never be given full outdoor sun. Move it into the shade outdoors, and keep it there.

## To Plunge or Not to Plunge?

Should you submerge your potted plants into the garden beds, or arrange them above ground? A pot submerged in garden soil will require less frequent watering. The cool earth surrounding the container will slow the evaporation rate, keeping the roots cooler and more moist. If you have an automatic irrigation system in place, you can position the potted specimens so the sprinklers or soaker hose water your houseplants. Additionally,

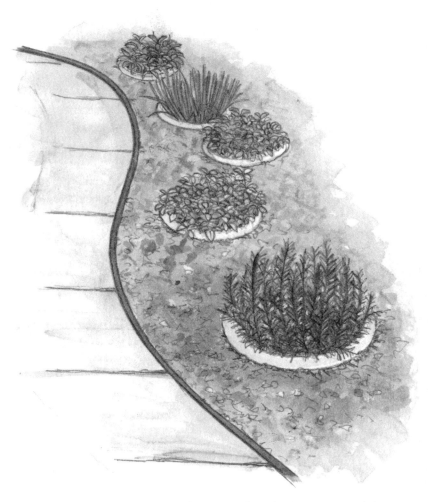

**BRING HOUSEPLANTS OUTDOORS** in summer, where they can act as annuals in your garden. Submerged potted plants will require less frequent watering.

your houseplants act as annuals, contributing to the beauty of your garden beds.

On the other hand, plants submerged in the garden are more vulnerable to pests of every variety, from deer and groundhogs to insects and slugs. Be sure not to submerge the lips of your pots. If you do, the plant may send roots out beyond its pot, which will make moving the plant back inside more difficult. As long as you can simply lift the pot and bring your plant indoors, there will be no root trauma.

Whether you've submerged your plants, hung them from the dappled light of your dogwood tree, or lined them up on the deck, check all houseplants for pests before bringing them back indoors. I keep mine in the garage for a few weeks so I can watch for problems and avoid spreading any pests or diseases through my collection.

Most plants benefit from a summer outdoors, and you'll appreciate the reduction in maintenance work. Summer rain does a nice job of watering your plants, and the elevated humidity of most temperate summer climates is well suited to our houseplants.

## Care When You're Away

Now, what if you want to go on vacation and leave your plants behind? There comes a time in every indoor gardener's life when she or he wants to travel, if only to visit gardens in other corners of the world. A 2-week absence isn't much to worry about, but if you need to leave town for 3 weeks or more, and you don't have a friend who owes you a big favor, there are a few things you can do to tide your plants over in your absence.

First, lower the temperature and turn down the lights. When I travel in winter, I leave the thermostats set to 55°F (13°C) and move plants away from the sunniest windows. This slows the rate of photosynthesis.

Second, group your plants together so they benefit from the increase in ambient humidity. As each plant transpires, the air surrounding the growing area becomes more humid, which means that less water moves from within the plant foliage to the surrounding air. I hang several poles across the top of my shower and fill the stall with hanging plants. Milk crates in the shower basin let me stack plants below.

To complete the scene, fill a plastic basin with water and leave it in the shower. Lift the toilet lid, fill the sink, close the door to the bathroom, and walk away. I can't promise you won't have a little mildew in the grout when you return, but arranged thusly, your plants will survive 3 to 4 weeks without you.

# MANAGING PESTS

THERE ARE A HANDFUL OF insect (and noninsect) pests that will snack on your houseplants, given half a chance. If you're vigilant, you can keep your indoor garden clean and healthy. It's impossible to avoid insects entirely, but a few sound practices will minimize problems.

Some people are reluctant to use pesticides in their homes because of the potential danger to children and pets. If you care for your plants well, you may never have to resort to commercial pesticides. Start with the least toxic method available. If it works, great. If not, you can either step up the attack or get rid of the plant and start fresh.

## Integrated Pest Management

Using the least toxic method is one of the key principles of Integrated Pest Management (IPM). This pest management strategy focuses on long-term prevention or suppression of pest problems through a combination of cultural, physical, and chemical tools to minimize health and environmental risks.

Begin by making the following five steps common practice:

1. Whenever you buy a new plant, isolate it for a week or two and watch carefully. Do not integrate it into your collection until you're sure it's free of pests.

2. Never buy a plant that isn't 100 percent clean and healthy. This doesn't mean you can't buy a plant that has a broken branch or a spent bloom stalk. Sometimes

it's possible to negotiate a good deal for a less-than-perfect specimen. But if you see an insect on the plant, just walk away.

3. Keep your growing areas neat and clean. Debris is a breeding ground for insects, so remove dead leaves and flowers as they fall. If you discover an infestation, clean the entire area thoroughly, including windowsills, windowpanes, and containers.

4. Pay attention to the cultural needs of your plants: temperature, light, food, and water. Plants are better able to survive an infestation when they're well grown and properly watered and fed, just as we are better able to fight off a cold when we're strong and well nourished.

5. Examine every plant in your collection at least once a week. It's essential to know what your plants look like when they're healthy, so you can spot a problem as soon as it occurs. Early detection is key; you can get rid of almost any pest if you catch it early enough.

I use nonchemical practices whenever possible. Products such as dishwashing liquid, mineral oil, and rubbing alcohol are extremely useful, and it's always a good idea to have a few bottles of beer on hand. The brew isn't meant to slake your thirst as you scout for aphids. Instead, it's both a lure and a solvent for slugs, the persistent mollusk capable of chewing large holes in your plants' foliage.

## Slugs

Slugs aren't usually household pests, but they can easily ride into your home on a plant from a greenhouse or nursery. Watch for the silvery trails they leave behind on plant leaves.

Slugs like a warm, moist environment, and your home is a safe haven without predators such as birds or toads. You may not catch them in the act because slugs are nocturnal creatures, but a few well-positioned saucers of beer work wonders. Place them near any houseplants that show signs of damage and wait. Slugs will find the beer, climb into the saucers to drink, and be dissolved by the liquid. Check your beer traps every morning and replenish them as needed. After a few weeks, you should be able to stop putting out bait.

## Spider Mites

Spider mites are another noninsect plant pest. This is not merely a technicality. Spider mites are arachnids (having eight legs, as opposed to six legs for insects), and they are susceptible to different chemicals than those that affect insects. However, the same cultural practices useful for combating insect infestations are effective against spider mites, too.

Spider mites are sucking pests. They suck the chlorophyll out of leaves, leaving behind dead, mottled leaf tissue. A speckled, pale leaf surface is often your first clue that mites are dining on your plant. Spider mites are also highly mobile. They may travel among plants under their own steam, or you may inadvertently transport them by brushing up against an infested leaf, then touching a clean plant. If you find spider mites on one plant, check its neighbors to see if they have spread.

Spider mites are particularly insidious because they are so hard to see. Webbing in the leaf axils or on the underside of leaves may be the first sign you'll see of an infestation. The easiest way to check for mites is by spraying water into the leaf axils. Mite webbing will catch the water droplets. Or tap the top of the leaf while holding it over a piece of paper. If small dots fall onto the paper, and if they move around, they are probably spider mites. You may need a magnifying glass to see them.

Don't confuse spider mites with spiders. Spider webs look different from spider mite webs; they are looser and more geometric in design. I welcome spiders among my plants (as long as they're not too large and scary) because they prey on insects.

If you have mites, there are several things to do. First, remove the damaged foliage and dispose of it. Second, assess the extent of the damage. Because spider mites are difficult to detect, they are often well established before we notice them. A large population can be tough to get rid of, and it may be better to get rid of the plant.

Mites are resistant to many pesticides, but if the infestation isn't advanced, try rubbing dishwashing liquid on both sides of your plant's foliage, covering all surfaces, and let it sit. After 15 to 20 minutes, rinse off the soap. Repeat this at 3-day intervals until you see no more sign of spider mites.

If the population of spider mites is large and you've decided to duke it out, you'll need something stronger than soap and water. A combination of systemic granular poison and liquid

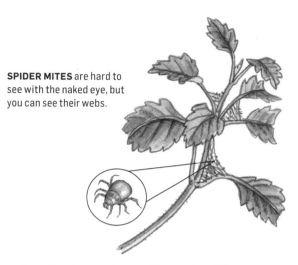

**SPIDER MITES** are hard to see with the naked eye, but you can see their webs.

spray can be effective against spider mites. The systemic granule is mixed into the soil where the plant absorbs it, making the plant itself poisonous to the mites. Systemic poisons take a while to be effective, which is why it's a good idea to use it in conjunction with a topical pesticide. Pyrethrum-based sprays are derived from plant chemicals (from *Tanacetum cinerariifolium*) and are not toxic to humans. Horticultural oils are also an excellent choice. Both sprays will kill mites on contact while the systemic poison is becoming established. Neither spray should be used when temperatures are above 75 to 80°F (24–27°C), as foliage may be damaged.

Once you've gotten mites under control, consider preventive measures: a rinse with cold, soapy water once every 2 or 3 weeks should keep spider mites from taking over. Small plants can be submerged in a washbasin filled with soapy water, while large specimens can be sprayed or washed by hand.

## Scale and Mealybugs

Scale is a sucking insect pest that can be difficult to detect. While the insects are visible to the naked eye, mature insects look like little brown dots and can be mistaken for bumps on bark, especially on ficus, citrus, and other woody plants. If you scrape a dot with your fingernail and it pops off, you have scale. The hard shell is a protective covering, under which lives a sucking insect. Most sprays are ineffective against scale because they cannot penetrate the shell.

If you've caught the problem early and the scale is not widespread, remove each insect with a cotton swab dipped in alcohol. If the infestation is widespread, this can be a tedious task.

Young insects are difficult to spot, but since they have not yet secreted their shell, they are vulnerable to spraying. After swabbing away the visible scale, spray the entire plant with a mixture of one part mineral oil, one part soap, and eight parts water. Test the solution on a single leaf first, to make sure it does not burn the foliage.

Mealybugs are a kind of soft scale. Instead of a hard, brown shell, they are protected by a waxy, white covering. There are several different kinds of mealybugs, but all are sucking insects and feed similarly to hard scale. Like scale, immature mealybugs are mobile and difficult to see, so plan a twofold attack. Remove the visible insects with a cotton swab and alcohol, then spray the foliage with the same soap/mineral oil/water solution recommended for scale.

**THE SHELL OF HARD SCALE** protects it from most insecticides.

**MEALYBUGS** are soft-scale insects. They have a cottony, waxy protective layer.

## Aphids

Aphids are a common insect pest that can reproduce with amazing speed. Aphids can both lay eggs and bear live young, and as a result, an infestation can reach epic proportions very quickly. Fortunately, aphids are pretty easy to kill.

If temperatures outside are warm, bring the afflicted plant outdoors and spray it with a blast of water from the hose. This will knock off most of the insects. If it's too cold to work outside, spray the plant with a solution of one part dishwashing liquid to nine parts water. Keep the plant separate from the rest of your plants for several weeks and continue treating the insects with soap and water. As with the other insect (and arachnid) pests we've discussed, the immature stages are small and difficult to see, so it will take several sessions before you've gotten rid of them all.

**APHIDS** usually feed on tender new growth.

## Other Pests

**Ants.** You may see ants on your plants, and while they don't attack plants per se, they may indicate a problem. Ants can act as shepherds to mealybugs, aphids, and scale. If you see a line of ants climbing up and down the stem of a plant, follow the trail; it may lead you to a colony of sucking insects. Also, look for a sticky liquid on the plant's leaves. This is called honeydew, and it's a sugar-rich substance excreted by sucking insects. Ants collect the honeydew, bring it back to their nest, and eat it.

**Sooty mold.** Sooty mold is a powdery black substance that grows on the surface of honeydew. It's easier to spot than the honeydew itself and can indicate the presence of an insect problem.

**Whitefly.** Whitefly is a pest that is easy to spot. Both adults and nymphs feed on the underside of tender leaves; when the foliage of a plant with white fly is touched, a cloud of insects

**SOOTY MOLD** grows on honeydew secretions and indicates an insect pest problem.

**WHITEFLIES** are a highly mobile plant pest and often ride in on new plants.

flies up into the air. In addition to feeding on your houseplants, whitefly can carry diseases from plant to plant. The adult stage is highly mobile and can spread through a plant collection quickly. You can control whitefly with the same solution of soap and water recommended for aphids (see page 70).

**Fungus gnats.** Indoor growers often complain of fruit flies around their houseplants. These are actually fungus gnats. Their larvae feed on organic matter in the potting mix and may occasionally damage root tissue. Established plants are not greatly affected by this, but seedlings may lose vigor. Fungus gnats prefer a moist, organic potting mix. Their population can be reduced by keeping the mix as dry as each individual plant will tolerate. This will kill the larvae and interrupt the reproductive cycle.

## Stronger Management Methods

There are times when stronger methods than IPM are required, and when used wisely, they are harmless to humans and pets and effective against pests. In addition to the horticultural oils and pyrethrum-based sprays mentioned above, neem oil is an especially interesting and effective pesticide. An organic pesticide derived from the neem tree (*Azadirachta indica*), it works against insects in several ways: as an antifeedant (preventing the ability to swallow), by interrupting the reproductive cycle, and by interfering with the molting necessary between developmental stages. Neem is effective against mites as well as insects, which makes it particularly useful to have on hand. And since it is less toxic than many pesticides (it can be used on food crops), this is an excellent choice if you need something stronger than soap and water.

At some point in your growing career, a plant pest will inevitably sneak into your home. If you pay close attention to your plants, you'll be able to identify the problem quickly and eliminate it, using the least toxic methods available.

# DISEASES

DISEASES ARE MORE DIFFICULT TO diagnose than pest infestations, but fortunately, they are also more rare. And many of the same good habits that keep your plants pest-free will also reduce their chances of acquiring a disease. Pathogens, which include fungi, bacteria, and viruses, cause most plant diseases.

## Preventive Measures

Quarantining a new plant is as important for preventing the spread of disease as it is for monitoring insect pests. Fungal and bacterial diseases can be spread by physical contact, so keep new acquisitions isolated for a week or two while you watch for signs of disease.

Check the health of each plant part before buying it. Make sure the leaves and stems are turgid and have healthy color. Feel and smell the potting mix. If it doesn't smell fresh and if the mix is wet, knock the plant out of its pot to examine the roots for rot. Rotten roots will be brown and wet; healthy roots will be white and plump.

At the risk of repeating myself, pay attention to the cultural needs of your plants: temperature, light, food, and water. Plants fight disease better when they're healthy and strong. If you're careless with maintenance, you may miss early indications of disease. As with insect pests, early detection is the key.

Pathogens enter plants through wounds, and washing the blade of your knife or scissors won't get rid of all microscopic organisms. Therefore, be careful when pruning and sterilize the blade before moving from plant to plant. This can be done by rinsing your blade in alcohol or holding your scissors over a flame.

## Fungi

Most plant diseases are caused by fungi, which reproduce via spores. A spore lands on a leaf; it may be airborne, splashed on with water, or deposited by direct physical contact. If water is present on the leaf, the spore will produce a hypha, a thread of fungus that penetrates plant tissue through stomata or wounds in plant tissue. Wound entry can be controlled to a certain degree by keeping the plant healthy and whole. And by maintaining a clean growing area, we can limit the chances that spores will penetrate through plant openings.

Pathogenic fungi kill plant cells and absorb the nutrients they need from those cells. Fungi don't have their own chlorophyll, so they can't photosynthesize (make their own food). Most fungi thrive in cool, wet conditions, so try not to leave standing water on plant foliage or flowers. Water early in the day so the water has time to dry before cooler evening temperatures provide the perfect breeding ground for fungus.

There are many symptoms of fungal diseases, but the most common is leaf spot. The spots can be black, brown, or gray. If you suspect a plant has a fungal disease, there's an easy way to find out. Cut off a piece of leaf with a spot and seal it in a ziplock bag. Put the bag someplace warm, say, on top of the refrigerator, and let it sit. After a week, take the leaf out of the bag and look at it with a magnifying glass. Do you see fungus growing out of the leaf spot? If so, your plant has a fungal disease. If you don't see fungus growing on the leaf spot, the plant may have a bacterial disease.

One of the most common and easily identifiable fungal diseases is botrytis, also known as gray mold. It can penetrate almost any soft part of a plant and cause bulb, stem, flower, leaf, or root rot. Botrytis produces copious fuzzy, gray spores. Infected cells turn rotten and mushy. Remove any plant parts with visible botrytis spores, improve air circulation, and eliminate standing water. Also, don't work with plants when the foliage is wet, to avoid spreading spores.

A diseased plant may infect its neighbors. If only a few leaves have been damaged, cut them off, then spray or dust the cut with a plant fungicide. If you don't have a fungicide on hand, sprinkle the cut with cinnamon, which makes an effective fungicide.

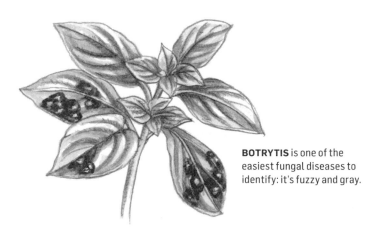

**BOTRYTIS** is one of the easiest fungal diseases to identify: it's fuzzy and gray.

## Bacteria

Some plant diseases are bacterial in nature. Bacteria are unicellular, much smaller than fungi, and undetectable to the naked eye. They too require a moist environment to thrive, and they also enter plant tissue through stomata and wounds.

Symptoms of bacterial diseases are similar to those of fungal diseases, including spots on foliage and flowers. If you've ruled out the possibility of a fungal disease, treat for bacteria. First, decide if your plant is worth saving. If so, cut off damaged parts and spray with Physan 20 or another antibacterial spray.

## Viruses

Viruses are transmitted through sap, or by tools, insects, or fingers. They cannot reproduce independently and can be seen only with an electron microscope. A virus can't function outside a cell; consider it a cell hijacker. Once inside the cell, the virus manipulates the host plant's internal cell structures to produce more viruses. Then the cell breaks open and sheds the viruses, and the cycle continues.

Viral plant diseases are relatively rare, which is fortunate since they are difficult to diagnose. Symptoms include stunted growth, a yellow mottling of the leaves, yellowing veins, or a pattern of yellow or greenish concentric rings or lines. Symptoms can be different in each plant, which makes diagnosis especially tough.

A plant can look perfectly healthy and still be infected. There is no cure for plant viruses, and they can be confirmed only by laboratory testing. Most reputable growers test for

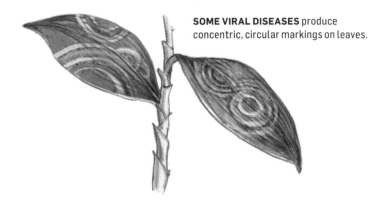

**SOME VIRAL DISEASES** produce concentric, circular markings on leaves.

viruses periodically, and as a result, viral diseases are not widespread among tropicals. Buy your plants from growers you can trust or who give you a guarantee. If you have an infected plant, get rid of it and the potting medium it was planted in. The pot itself may be reused after soaking it for an hour in a solution of 1 cup bleach in 1 gallon of water.

It can take time for disease symptoms to manifest themselves. Not only is it sometimes impossible to identify a plant disease until damage has already been done, but once you detect the symptoms, it can be difficult to pinpoint the problem. Because plant diseases are fairly rare in individual collections, this shouldn't worry you. Pay attention, and give your plants the excellent care that will keep them strong and disease resistant.

# PART THREE

# DESIGNING THE INDOOR GARDEN

A thoughtful indoor landscape brings color, interest, and life to any home.

## IT'S ALL IN THE DISPLAY

ONCE YOU'RE HOOKED on indoor gardening, you're going to want to get creative with your display. Not that there's anything wrong with a simple pot on a windowsill, but there are many more interesting ways to show off your indoor garden.

### Grow Vertical!

My New York apartment has a single window that faces a brick wall. Not a great view, but I make the most of it by turning the window into a hanging garden. Since my window is dark (remember the brick wall across the way), I framed the window with banks of fluorescent tubes, screwing the fixtures into the frame, then masking them with a window treatment.

You may create your own combination of poles and shelves, or purchase a set of hanging Plexiglas shelves built expressly for window gardening. In either case, clear glass or Plexiglas allows for maximum light to pass through to the plants on lower shelves. A pole hung above the top of the window frame provides space for hanging plants, while shelves across the window itself are for potted specimens.

If you're going to grow hanging plants, you need hanging baskets. Mostly they come in plastic, but you can turn any pot into a hanging pot by attaching a metal clip-on hanger. These hold a lot of weight and clip easily onto the edges of clay pots or the saucers underneath them. They come in several standard lengths and are inexpensive. Hangers made from fishing line and Plexiglas hold less weight but have the advantage of being almost invisible. These are better suited for lightweight plastic and fiberglass pots.

Most plastic hanging baskets have reservoirs built in to the bottom and snap-on trays to catch runoff. Still, it's a good idea to tip your baskets over the sink after you water, pouring off excess water from the saucers before re-hanging your plants.

Plastic baskets are easy to lift overhead and generally don't require much hardware to install, since they're lighter than clay. They're not beautiful, but since the foliage of your hanging houseplant cascades downward, it should screen out most of the basket.

## Mini Rainforest

If you're committed to growing plants that require high humidity, consider planting a terrarium. A simple aquarium is a good place to start. An aquarium can be planted with soil or used to display a collection of individual potted plants. In every case, it's important not to crowd the tank. If plants are placed too close together, air can't circulate among them and the risk of disease increases. Moist, still air and standing water (even in small drops) facilitate the spread of diseases. Also, make sure that plant foliage doesn't touch the glass sides. Wet foliage can burn when the light focuses on it through the glass.

First, place a layer of gravel on the bottom of the tank to provide drainage. The depth of this layer is determined by the depth of the aquarium. A 15-gallon tank should have a gravel layer 1 to 1½ inches deep. Next, add premoistened, lightweight potting mix. Premoistened soil is easier and neater to work with and can be made by pouring your potting mix into a large plastic container, adding water, and letting it sit overnight to absorb moisture. The depth of the soil layer will depend on the size of your tank. A 15-gallon tank should have a soil layer of 2 to 3 inches deep.

**A TERRARIUM** can be a showcase for your plants and raise humidity for delicate specimens.

The placement of your plants is up to you, although it makes sense to place the tallest plants at the back of the case. If the display will be viewed from all sides, plant your tallest specimens in the center. When you've finished planting, water sparingly to allow the roots of each plant to make good contact with the soil around it. Do not allow water to accumulate in the tank above the drainage layer. This will lead to rot and ruin.

If you choose to use your aquarium to house individual pots, first place a layer of gravel in the bottom of the tank. Place your pots on the gravel, and if you'd like to vary the heights of your plants, place a few pots on top of flat rocks or overturned pots. Add water to the bottom of your aquarium, up to the level of the gravel. As with a dry well, the pots shouldn't sit in water.

A glass or plastic terrarium cover will let light in but keep moisture from escaping. In this highly humid environment, it's important to watch for signs of diseases or pests, which might thrive in humid air. While you will only need to water a closed terrarium infrequently (once every 2 to 4 weeks), you should check its general health at least once a week.

If your terrarium lives in a bay window, you probably won't need to add artificial light, but if you place your terrarium in a dark spot, you can use an overhead fish tank–type fixture as a light source. However, many fluorescent tubes labeled for aquariums are strongest in the yellow/green wavelengths, which is not especially useful for plants. Instead, choose full-spectrum fluorescent tubes that will fit your fixture or tubes that are strongest in the red and blue wavelengths.

## Think Outside the Pot

Almost anything can hold a plant, and the more creative you get, the more interesting your plant collection will look. I ask but one thing: until you get *really* good at this, make sure every container has a drainage hole in the bottom. (I've seen far too many potted orchids rot in place because no one realized they were drowning in their glass vases.) If you find a gorgeous antique porcelain bowl and can't bear to drill holes in it, you can still use the pot . . . just make it a cachepot (that's French for hide-pot). Pot your houseplant in a container with drainage holes, then place the entire pot into your fancy container. This way you can see when the plant has had enough water and can pour the excess out of the cachepot.

But why stop there? The cachepot offers way more possibilities. If you have a moisture-loving plant that would grow best in a nonporous material like plastic, or if you simply don't have time to water except on weekends and need to stretch the interval between waterings, you can pot your houseplant in plastic (which, though not necessarily beautiful, does have the advantage of maintaining soil moisture), then camouflage it by slipping the whole thing into a cachepot. A wicker basket, a piece of art pottery, a set of old mixing bowls: you name it . . . it's a cachepot.

Or think outside the pot entirely. The craziest display I ever came up with was purely whimsical: three styrofoam wig heads planted with houseplants.

To make mine, I started with a 3-inch drill bit (sometimes called a hole saw bit) and cut a hole 2 to 3 inches deep into the top center of the head, creating my planter. Then I drilled a 1-inch hole through the bottom of the planter section into the hollow neck of the wig head. This provided drainage. I spray-painted mine with a terra-cotta-colored paint, but you can choose any color you like. After the paint dried, I placed a small piece of landscape cloth (you could also use a terra-cotta pottery shard) over the drainage hole and potted my plant. With wig heads, the foliage suggests hair. A snake plant becomes a fright wig, standing straight up in the air. A spider plant looks like long, bushy hair, and a burro's tail becomes dreadlocks.

I realize a line of planted heads may not be everyone's taste. But how about a rainbow assortment of enamel coffee-pots, a row of 1920s art pottery, a kid's dump truck, an old tea set, a pair of hiking boots, an antique bird cage, a Victrola from the 1960s, a group of blue glass mason jars, slogan coffee mugs, a 1940s milk bottle carrier, or vintage cocktail shakers? There's got to be something in that list that sounds interesting to you!

# FOLIAGE

FOLIAGE IS THE BACKBONE of every garden, indoors or out. When you choose a combination of interesting leaf shapes, sizes, and colors, you are literally designing with foliage. The patterns are always changing, always growing, and always wonderful. These 10 plants offer a wide range of foliage styles. There's something for everyone.

## Bromeliads

Bromeliads are a group of tropical plants with foliage that grows in a basal rosette. Brightly colored bracts (which are actually modified leaves) and small flowers emerge from a reservoir in the center of the leaves. In nature, these are understory plants that grow in the dappled light of the forest floor. The reservoir collects water and nutrients for the plant. In your home, they'll

Earth star bromeliad

be happy in almost any exposure, depending on the species. They are generally very drought tolerant, although they appreciate the elevated humidity of a dry well. Grow them in a fast-draining, soilless mix, and fill the reservoir once a week.

An excellent small bromeliad for a northern or eastern exposure is the earth star (*Cryptanthus* spp.). Its leaves are arranged in a star pattern, and its foliage is green, striped in red or white depending on the species. Larger bromeliads, such as *Aechmeas* and *Neoregelias*, bloom best in western or southern light. Their bracts and flowers can last for 6 to 8 weeks, after which the plant slowly begins to die. Before they expire, most bromeliads will produce several offsets, which gradually replace the parent plant.

## Climbing Onions (*Bowiea volubilis*)

This plant couldn't be easier to grow, and its unusual growth habit makes it a great focal point for any indoor garden. Bulbs grow half in, half out of the soil, and flexible, finely branched stems emerge from the top of each bulb. In nature, the bulbs go dormant; stems turn yellow, then brown, then die back until the rainy season prompts more growth. In the average home, bulbs may never go dormant, but if they do, water no more than once a week until you see new growth emerge from the top of a bulb.

The bright, indirect light of a northern or eastern window is fine, although the plant will not flower without the direct sun of a western or southern exposure. The flowers of climbing onion are small and insignificant; most people grow this plant for its outstanding foliage. Stems can be trained on an upright form or allowed to trail. This is a very drought-tolerant plant, as the basal bulbs store water for times of drought in nature. Water only when the top inch of soil is dry. The climbing onion grows best in a fast-draining, soilless mix.

## Crotons (*Codiaeum variegatum*)

This showy plant requires moist soil, full sun, and high humidity. If you have a southern exposure that can accommodate a dry well, try a croton for a year-round blast of color. Its foliage is shiny and comes in several shapes and a variety of patterns and colors. Green leaves may be spotted or striped with yellow, orange, red, or purple. Direct sun keeps the variegation intense, so even though you can grow this plant in bright, indirect light, the colors may be more muted.

Water your croton when the soil surface is dry to the touch, and grow it in potting soil, which retains moisture longer than a soilless mix. If you notice leaves starting to drop, that means the plant is too dry or too cold (below 60°F/16°C) or isn't getting enough humidity. Check your growing conditions and make adjustments.

# Ferns

Most people think of ferns as delicate, difficult creatures, yet many are low-maintenance houseplants that tolerant a wide range of growing conditions. Footed ferns are an especially hardy group. Furry rhizomes grow at soil level, sending roots down and stems up. As understory plants in nature, these ferns grow well in northern and eastern windows. In a very bright room, they can be grown several feet in from the windows.

The rabbit's foot fern (*Phlebodium aureum*) produces deeply lobed, blue-green leaves that are 1 to 3 feet tall. It's graceful and sculptural and surprisingly drought tolerant. Water when the top ½ inch of potting mix feels dry. Squirrel's foot fern (*Davallia fejeensis*) is a smaller plant with finely cut foliage that reaches 12 to 18 inches in length. In a hanging basket, the rhizomes will eventually circle the pot, sending foliage in every direction to form a ball of fern. It, too, should be watered only when the top ½ inch of soil feels dry.

**Rabbit's foot fern**

## Mosaic Plants (*Fittonia verschaffeltii*)

This little plant fits on even the smallest windowsill. Dark green leaves are heavily veined with pink or white and maintain their variegation even in low light. The mosaic plant grows best in a northern or eastern window and appreciates high humidity, so grow it on a dry well. This is a moisture-loving plant; it should be grown in a soil-based mix and watered when the soil surface feels dry. When the mosaic plant gets too dry, its leaves and stems droop dramatically. If you catch it quickly (within a day), it will perk right up again, but if this happens repeatedly, it can stress the plant.

The mosaic plant roots easily from cuttings. If your plant gets too leggy, simply pinch off the tip of the plant (including a few pairs of leaves) and stick the pieces in the pot, next to the parent plant.

## Philodendrons

Philodendrons are often considered commonplace, but they are such easy, obliging houseplants that they deserve a mention. Some are also significantly beautiful. As understory plants in nature, they are well suited to the light of a northern or eastern window. If you have only bright sun, grow philodendrons behind a sheer curtain or at the center of the room. These plants are drought-tolerant vines that thrive on benign neglect.

Split-leaf philodendron (*Philodendron bipinnatifidum*) is an impressive plant that can fill a bay window all by itself. Its foliage is large, lobed, and a glossy, deep green. It grows best in a soilless mix; water when the top inch of potting mix feels dry. This plant is a large, living sculpture and deserves to be a focal point in the indoor garden.

Only have a small sill? Satin pothos (*Scindapsus pictus*) is pretty much bulletproof as long as you don't let it freeze or drown. Heart-shaped, medium-green leaves are outlined and flecked with silver; so much prettier than plain old pothos. Grow this in a hanging basket to fully appreciate the graceful drape of its foliage.

Satin pothos

## Prayer Plants (*Maranta* spp.)

This is a group of plants with outstanding foliar variegation; markings of red, pink, and several shades of green look like they were painted onto each leaf. The common name comes from the fact that in the dark, prayer plant leaves move from a horizontal to a vertical position, which some devout gardener thought looked like praying hands. It can be grown either in a hanging basket or on a tabletop or windowsill.

Prayer plants should be watered when the soil surface feels dry. They grow best in high humidity, so place them on dry wells to avoid brown leaf margins, especially in the dry air of winter. While prayer plants thrive in bright, indirect light (an east or west window), they'll also grow in an unobstructed north-facing window. It's unusual to find a plant with such extraordinary variegation that tolerates low light levels.

## Rex Begonias (*Begonia rex*)

Some begonias are grown for their flowers and others for their foliage. Rex begonias (literally the kings of begonias!) have gorgeous leaves, painted with fantastic swirls of color (greens, whites, pinks, silvers, and purples). These begonias are rhizomatous. A thick rhizome grows partially exposed at soil level; roots grow down and stems grow up from nodes along the rhizome.

Rex begonias like to dry out a little between watering, so water when the top ½ inch of soil feels dry. They grow best in bright, indirect light and high humidity. If you see browning along the leaf margins, don't compensate with more frequent watering. This is a sign that humidity is too low, so place your rex begonia on a dry well. Grow rex begonias in a soilless mix.

## Ribbon Bushes (*Homalocladium platycladum*)

The structure of this plant is fascinating. Green stems are segmented and flat and about 1 inch wide. There are small leaves that drop fairly quickly, leaving the stems to photosynthesize. Small, greenish flowers form directly on the stems and are followed by dark purple fruit. Ribbon bush grows quickly and tolerates a wide range of exposures. It may not flower in a northern window, but the flowers aren't the most interesting thing about this plant, so really, who cares?

This plant is relatively new to the houseplant market and until recently was a rare curiosity. It makes an excellent specimen plant because of its quick rate of growth and unique form. It grows happily in either soilless or soil-based mixes and should be watered when the top ½ inch of soil feels dry.

## Snake Plants (*Sansevieria* spp.)

Snake plants are succulent plants with rosettes of stiff foliage that come in a range of sizes and colors. All are quite drought tolerant and should be grown in a quick-draining, soilless mix. Water only when the mix feels dry 1 inch below the surface. You may be familiar with the most common snake plant, *Sansevieria trifasciata*. Its long leaves are highly sculptural. A line of three or four well-grown specimens in matching pots is a beautiful thing. This obliging tropical plant tolerates every exposure.

For a little more color, try Mother-in-law's tongue (*S. trifasciata* 'Laurentii'). This variety has yellow leaf margins that contrast nicely with the dark green center. *S. trifasciata* 'Moonshine' has slightly wider, silvery-green leaves. If you need a smaller plant, try a bird's nest *Sansevieria* such as 'Gold Hahnii'. Its yellow and green leaves are only 6 to 10 inches tall.

**Mother-in-law's tongue**

# FLOWERING PLANTS

IT'S DISCOURAGING TO buy a plant that's in flower, only to find you can't get it to rebloom in your home growing conditions. Plants often need high light to produce flowers, and the light they get in the greenhouse where they were raised was probably considerably higher than what most of us can provide at home. The following plants really (really!) do bloom well in the average living space. Don't expect windowsills full of bloom; think of the flowers as the stars of your indoor garden. Position them where they'll have the most impact when they're at their best, and when they've finished blooming, move them back into the chorus line.

## African Violets (*Saintpaulia ionantha*)

African violets are old-fashioned houseplants: dependable, easygoing, and easy to propagate. Don't for a minute think this means they're boring and not worth growing. Flowers come in a range of saturated colors, and new hybrids sport splashy, variegated foliage. The stems and leaves are somewhat succulent, and the plant can tolerate moderate drought. The foliage is velvety and should be kept dry; water on the foliage may leave spots. You may water carefully from above, or water from below, allowing water to be absorbed up through the potting mix. Pour any excess out of the saucer.

Grow African violets in bright, indirect light, and water when the top ½ inch of potting mix feels dry. This is one of the few houseplants that will bloom in a north-facing window (as long as it's not obstructed). Variegated varieties require brighter light than green-leafed African violets. In lower light, the leaves may revert to green. This plant grows best in a lightweight, soilless potting mix; heavy soil will lead to root rot.

## Begonias (*Begonia* species)

The genus *Begonia* is large and varied, and many are reliable bloomers. Angel wing begonias are some of the easiest begonias to flower indoors and are also popular bedding plants in the outdoors. In fact, if you have angel wings in your garden and the first frost is approaching, why not pot them up and try them as houseplants? It's better than throwing them away.

Angel wing begonias have succulent stems and leaves grouped in opposite pairs that look like (you guessed it) angel wings. They'll bloom best in bright, indirect light and are fairly drought tolerant. Water when the top ½ inch of soil is dry. Foliage may be plain green or have white spots or stripes. Flowers come in shades of white and pink.

Angel wing begonia

## Citrus

Citrus plants not only give us fragrant blooms but also ornamental (and tasty) fruit. They grow best in full sun; an unobstructed south-facing window is perfect. Citrus are more cold tolerant than many other houseplants. In nature, these are subtropical and tropical plants. They also grow best if allowed to dry out a little between waterings. Water when the soil feels dry down to your first knuckle (about 1 inch deep).

Calamondin orange (*Citrofortunella mitis*) and kumquats (*Fortunella margarita*) are the two easiest citrus to bloom and grow indoors. The fruit of both is small and ripens to a rich, bright orange color. Both are edible, and you can even eat the skin of the kumquat. The calamondin orange is supertart and better for marmalade than for eating plain. Ripe fruit will remain edible and in good shape on the plant for several months.

Calamondin orange

## Clivia (*Clivia miniata*)

Clivias offer a bang of brilliance at the end of winter, when you really appreciate the color. Most plants have orange flowers, but some rarer cultivars have yellow blooms. It grows best in a soilless potting mix and is quite drought tolerant. Water when the top inch of mix feels dry. Clivias bloom best when potbound, so there's no need to worry about frequent repotting. Dark green, straplike foliage is attractive year-round.

Grow clivia in bright, indirect light. This is another subtropical plant (from a frost-free temperate zone). It will grow and bloom best when placed in a cool location (45 to 50°F [7–10°C]) for several months (think unheated bedroom, garage, or cellar). Also, during this rest period, water no more than once every 2 weeks until you see the flower spike appear. If your clivia flowers, but the bloom is compressed between the leaves of the plant, you are not letting it get cold enough during its rest period.

## Crown of Thorns (*Euphorbia milii*)

This plant provides both cheerful flowers and an interesting, sculptural form. Crown of thorns grows best in bright, indirect light to full sun; you'll get more flowers with more sun. It's a drought-tolerant plant and should be watered when the potting mix feels dry down to your first knuckle. A soilless potting mix is best for this plant, providing the quick drainage it prefers. Crown of thorns grows well in a small container, which is fortunate because it sulks for a while after repotting.

Crown of thorns is a close relative of the poinsettia and shares several of its characteristics. What we think of as the flowers are actually showy bracts surrounding very small, yellow flowers. These bracts may be white, pink, red, or yellow, depending on the cultivar. Also, like the poinsettia, crown of thorns exudes a white, milky sap when broken. This may irritate sensitive skin, so handle with care. Crown of thorns is not a cactus, but look out for the thorns that give it its name.

## Flamingo Flowers (*Anthurium* spp.)

Favorites in floral arrangements, flamingo flowers are also easygoing houseplants. They have shiny, heart-shaped leaves and dramatic flowers composed of a spathe and a spadix. Flowers may be white, pink, or variegated, and are quite dramatic. They grow best in a consistently moist soil, so water when the top of the potting mix feels dry to the touch.

Flamingo flowers grow best in bright, indirect light with just a little direct sun; an unobstructed east window is perfect. Too much direct sun may cause leaves to burn. This plant appreciates high humidity, so grow it on a dry well for best results. As the plant ages, it produces new crowns around the central crown. These can be separated from the parent plant and potted up on their own for easy propagation.

## Lipstick Plants (*Aeschynanthus* spp.)

Lipstick plants are so named because someone thought the flowers looked like bright-colored lipsticks poking out of their tubes. I think their flowers are much more beautiful than that. *Aeschynanthus radicans* has cherry-red flowers emerging from a deep red calyx, and *A. speciosus* has even larger brilliant orange flowers. The foliage of both has a cascading growth habit; this is a plant to grow in a hanging basket or perched on a plant stand where the foliage can fall freely.

Grow lipstick plants in an eastern or western window where they'll get lots of bright, indirect light. These are drought-tolerant plants with a waxy cuticle; water when the potting mix feels dry about ½ inch down. They'll grow best in a soilless potting mix that drains quickly. Lipstick plants are gesneriads (so are African violets). This group of plants is sensitive to cold water; watering with cold water can cause leaf spot.

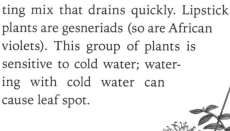

## Moth Orchids (*Phalaenopsis* spp.)

How is it possible that such an exotic, enchanting flower can be so easy to grow, so easy to find, and so inexpensive? Moth orchids are low-maintenance, drought-tolerant houseplants with showy flowers that can last for months at a time. It may sound too good to be true, but it isn't. Flowers come in a wide range of colors and patterns, from simple and sophisticated to bright and busy. They grow best in bright, indirect light; direct sun can burn their leaves.

Most moth orchids are killed with kindness. Remember, its succulent foliage and waxy cuticle indicate this is a drought-tolerant plant. If your orchid is potted in bark, water no more than once a week. If it's potted in long-grain sphagnum moss, once every 10 to 14 days is plenty. If you notice the lower leaves turning yellow, dial back your watering frequency.

## Stephanotis (*Stephanotis floribunda*)

Stephanotis flowers grow in clusters of bright white, tubular, and very fragrant blooms. This is a vining plant, but since stems can get very long, it's better to grow it trained on a trellis or teepee rather than in a hanging basket. While stephanotis doesn't flower year-round, you'll get several months-long bloom seasons each year, and its stiff, dark green leaves are always attractive.

Stephanotis grows best in very bright, indirect light or full sun. Try it in a southern or western window. If you notice bleached or burned spots on the leaves, pull it back from the window. This is a drought-tolerant plant and needs water only when the top inch of potting mix is dry.

## Wax Plants (*Hoya* spp.)

These vining plants grow well in hanging baskets, where their succulent leaves and star-shaped, fragrant blooms can be appreciated from all angles. The flower size is variable, from the ¼-inch-wide blooms of *Hoya lacunosa* to the 1-inch bloom of *H. onychoides*. Most of the wax plants you'll find in garden centers have fragrant blooms in shades of pink, with individual flowers about ½ inch wide.

Wax plants grow best in bright, indirect light or full sun. Flowers form on existing bloom spurs, so leave them in place once the flowers drop. Grow these plants in a soilless mix and water when the top inch of soil feels dry; these are drought-tolerant plants. Leaves may be solid green or variegated with white or pink. *H. carnosa* (the most readily available wax plant) can tolerate drafts to 50°F (10°C).

# TREES

SOMETIMES YOU WANT a plant with a big presence and an imposing structure — something like a tree. Here are five suggestions for plants that grow well indoors.

## Aralias (*Polyscias* spp.)

These trees have delicate foliage on long, flexible stems. Stems may need to be staked if they grow to exceed 3 or 4 feet. The leaves of ming aralia (*Polyscias fruticosa*) are finely dissected, while those of the unfortunately named chicken gizzard aralia (*P. crispata*) have glossy, round leaflets. Both are highlight plants and grow best in a western or southern window, although they'll tolerate eastern light.

Aralias do not appreciate a draft and will drop leaves in temperatures below 55°F (13°C). Water when the top ½ inch of soil feels dry, and if possible, grow on a dry well. You can prune aralias to keep them table size, but they are truly glorious when allowed to grow into tree form.

Ming aralia

## Ficus Alii (*Ficus bennendijkii* 'Alii')

A close relative of the familiar weeping fig, this plant is easier to grow and more beautiful. Its leaves are 3 to 8 inches long, slim, and pointy. While *Ficus benjamina* (weeping fig) has a reputation for dropping its leaves when it gets too cold or too dry, *F.* 'Alii' is less temperamental. It grows best in bright, indirect light and should only be watered when the top inch of soil feels dry.

As a young plant, 'Alii' has leaves along the entire length of its stem. With age, the lower leaves drop and the plant reveals its trunk. It's an imposing tree with both grace and substance.

## Lady Palms (*Rhapis excelsa*)

All palms have delicate fronds, but the lady palm has especially interesting foliage. Its fan-shaped fronds are slightly pleated, glossy, and dark green, with notched tips that look as though they were cut with pinking shears. Its stems are covered with a dark brown fiber.

It grows best in a soil-based mix and bright, indirect light; full sun can cause its leaves to turn yellow. Water when the top inch of potting mix feels dry. Keep your lady palm on a dry well when possible; leaf margins may turn brown in low humidity. If this happens, trim them with pinking shears to maintain their unique shape. Lady palm is a slow grower. A mature specimen is something special.

## Pencil Cactus (*Euphorbia tirucalli*)

This succulent plant is not only interesting to look at, but it's also unusual from a physiological point of view. Small leaves drop off after a few weeks, leaving the stiff, green stems to photosynthesize. These stems branch every 6 to 8 inches, creating a complex, interwoven structure that is both delicate and commanding.

Pencil cactus (not a real cactus) grows in almost every exposure. In full sun, stems may take on a reddish hue. Plant it in a soilless mix, and water when the top inch of soil feels dry. Remember, this is a true succulent and quite drought tolerant. Small plants can be grown on a windowsill, and large specimens can grow to be 6 feet tall in containers.

## Umbrella Trees (*Schefflera* spp.)

The umbrella tree (*Schefflera actinophylla*) is one of the easiest large tropicals to grow indoors. It grows best in bright, indirect light and a soilless mix. Water when the top inch of potting mix feels dry. The leaves of the umbrella tree are composed of seven or more leaflets, which radiate out from a central point. Foliage may be solid green or splashed with yellow or cream, depending on the cultivar.

Umbrella trees can get quite large. If you have a healthy specimen, you'll need to prune it every few years to keep it in bounds. *Schefflera arboricola* is a smaller species of umbrella tree that requires identical care. Both grow well in the average home as long as they're kept away from temperature extremes (drafty windows and hot radiators).

# CACTI

CACTI MAKE GREAT HOUSEPLANTS, as long as you understand their specific cultural needs. There are two kinds of cacti: desert and jungle. Yes, jungle, as in tropical rainforest. Not what you expected, is it? Jungle cacti are epiphytes. They live perched in trees and are quite drought tolerant. In the home, most require watering every 7 to 10 days. They are among the easiest of houseplants.

## Holiday Cacti (*Schlumbergera* spp.)

Christmas cactus, Thanksgiving cactus — call them what you will, these holiday cacti are some of the easiest, most rewarding cacti you can grow. A flush of bloom lasts for several weeks, although individual flowers only last for 3 to 7 days, depending on the temperature. Water your holiday cacti when

the top inch of soil is dry, and grow them in a soilless mix and bright, indirect light.

The stems of holiday cacti consist of succulent segments about 1 inch long. Tubular flowers may be white, red, or shades of pink. Flowering is triggered by the number of daylight hours and the temperature. To set buds, these cacti need cool temperatures and several weeks of 12 to 16 hours of darkness each day. I keep mine outdoors in fall until nighttime temps are around 50°F (10°C), then I bring them inside and watch them bloom.

## Cacti Watering Needs

As you might expect, desert cacti are even more drought tolerant than jungle cacti. In winter, many desert cacti can go four weeks between waterings, depending on the type and growing conditions. These full-sun plants are as drought tolerant as they come, but that doesn't mean they don't need *any* water. If you notice your cactus looking wrinkled or shriveled, increase the frequency with which you water.

The spines of cacti are modified leaves, and the succulent cacti bodies are modified stems that evolved to store water efficiently. Many cacti bloom best after a cool rest period in winter. Keep them between 50 and 55°F (10–13°C), and water only every 4 weeks. Cactus flowers are often large in proportion to their bodies, but even when they're not in bloom, cacti are fascinating to look at, with their intricate patterns of ridges and spines. Why some growers persist in gluing straw flowers to the top of cacti is beyond me. Do they think they can improve on nature?

## Mistletoe Cacti (*Rhipsalis* spp.)

These may not look like cacti, but they are. Like holiday cacti, they have stems that photosynthesize, and also like holiday cacti, they grow best in hanging baskets where their cascading growth habit can be appreciated. Grow them in soilless mix and bright, indirect light, and water when the top inch of soil feels dry.

Mistletoe cacti are so named because their flowers are followed by small berries, either red or white, like mistletoe. The decorative fruit lingers on the stems for up to 1 year. These cacti don't require any manipulations of temperature or light to bloom. Stems can be smooth or hairy, pencil-thick or thin as string. Too much water or too little light will cause them to drop pieces of stem.

## Orchid Cacti (*Epiphyllum* spp.)

These cacti are native to the rainforest, where many of them grow perched in trees. As plants that grow in the shade of trees, they are well suited to bright, indirect light indoors. Although they are drought tolerant, they need water more often than desert cacti. Grow them in a soilless mix, and water when the top inch of soil feels dry.

Photosynthetic stems are flat; some have spines, and some do not. The stems branch at nodes, giving them an asymmetrical shape. Some are hanging plants, and others are upright. While the structure of these plants is interesting, the flowers will stop you in your tracks. They can be 8 inches in diameter and come in white, yellow, red, or pink.

## Golden Barrel Cactus (*Echinocactus grusonii*)

As its common name suggests, this cactus has a stout, barrel-shaped body covered with a thick layer of golden spines. The highly ornamental spines are also curved and sharp; bear that in mind when choosing a spot for the plant. Only larger, older species flower, but since the spines are so decorative, it hardly matters.

This full-sun plant grows relatively quickly for a cactus and can make an impressive specimen as it ages and produces multiple barrels. Over-watering will cause the barrels to rot. Start out watering once a month; if you notice any shriveling, increase your watering frequency to once every 3 weeks. Grow this plant in cactus mix and a porous clay pot.

## Pincushion Cacti (*Mammillaria* spp.)

This is a large group of small, rounded cacti that are well suited to windowsill growing. Like most desert cacti, they require plenty of direct sun to flower. Unlike many desert cacti, pincushion cacti will flower when they're only a few years old. Blooms often form a circle around the top of the cactus, and if pollinated, the flowers are followed by red berries, which remain ornamental for months.

A pincushion cactus may bloom even without a cool winter rest, although perhaps with fewer individual blooms. Grow it in a soilless potting mix or cactus mix in a porous pot and full sun.

## Sea Urchin Cacti (*Echinopsis* spp.)

This is one of the easiest cacti to get to flower indoors. Put it in a sunny spot, water once a month, and that's it. If you can keep it cool in winter (50 to 55°F [10–13°C]), even better. Grow it in a porous clay pot and a soilless mix or special cactus mix.

Flowers emerge from furry buds and open into giant (8-inch-long), showy, trumpet-shaped blooms in white and pink, depending on the species. This is a slow grower, so you won't need to repot often. Sea urchin cacti start out barrel-shaped, but elongate as they mature, becoming cylindrical.

# INDEX

Page numbers in *italic* indicate illustrations; page numbers in **bold** indicate charts.

rubbing alcohol, 36

# OTHER STOREY TITLES YOU WILL ENJOY

## *Bonsai Survival Manual* by Colin Lewis

Grow attractive bonsai and keep them healthy with this "one-stop" source
of vital information. From evaluating and selecting plants to assessing plant
health and troubleshooting, *Bonsai Survival Manual* provides the comprehen-
sive information you need for success. The book includes advice on
selecting suitable species; feeding, watering, and providing the proper
temperature; step-by-step guidance on keeping your miniature tree in
shape and avoiding common bonsai ailments; and detailed horticultural
profiles of 50 popular commercial varieties, with at-a-glance information
on their specific requirements.
160 pages. Paper. ISBN 978-0-88266-853-6.

## *The Complete Houseplant Survival Manual* by Barbara Pleasant

Do you love the idea of having houseplants but find that they tend to die
in your care? Have you ever received a gift of a gorgeous flowering pot that
you can't identify and have no idea how to keep alive? Or maybe you're
already a houseplant enthusiast, ready to expand your knowledge — as well
as your plant collection. Barbara Pleasant covers these situations and more
in her friendly approach to selecting and caring for indoor plants. With personality profiles, growing needs, and troubleshooting tips for 160 blooming
and foliage varieties, you'll never kill another houseplant.
384 pages. Flexibind. ISBN 978-1-58017-569-2.

These and other books from Storey Publishing are available
wherever quality books are sold or by calling 1-800-441-5700.
Visit us at *www.storey.com* or sign up for our newsletter
at *www.storey.com/signup*.